THE
LITTLE
BOOK
OF
CHESHIRE

ROGER STEPHENS

The
History
Press

First published 2018

The History Press
97 St George's Place,
Cheltenham, Gloucestershire, GL50 3QB
www.thehistorypress.co.uk

British Library Cataloguing in Publication Data.
A catalogue record for this book is available from the British Library.

ISBN 978 0 7509 8596 3

Typesetting and origination by The History Press
Printed and bound in Great Britain by TJ International Ltd

CONTENTS

INTRODUCTION

'What a land of history, romance and beauty this Cheshire is! Will some wizard ever write of it as Scott wrote of the borderland?'

Fletcher Moss (1842–1919)

To cram all that history, romance and beauty into a book this size would be wizardry indeed! I have chosen, therefore, a miscellany of topics from Cheshire's story that will be of interest to 'frem folk' as well as natives.

If it requires a dedicatee, I might choose a teacher from my days at Hartford Primary School. One day, she set our class the task of listing things that Cheshire is famous for, and I incurred her wrath because I could only think of seven or eight, while most of my classmates listed so many that they were calling for extra sheets of paper. In her eyes, I was either too lazy or not proud enough, or both.

So, Mrs Taylor, if you can hear me from the Elysian Fields, all I can say is that, having lived my whole life in Cheshire, lack of pride is no longer a problem, even if laziness still is.

Miss! I've thought of some more!

Roger Stephens, 2018

1

HISTORY

BOUNDARY PEOPLE

It could all have turned out so differently.

When, in AD 79, the Roman army reached the mouth of the Dee it must have seemed like the ideal place to establish a fortress. Not only were they driving a wedge between the northern Brigantes and the Cornovii of the Midlands, but they would also control important trade routes and have a port for Ireland and beyond. Dewa (later to become the city of Chester) was built, like other Roman strongholds, in the shape of a playing

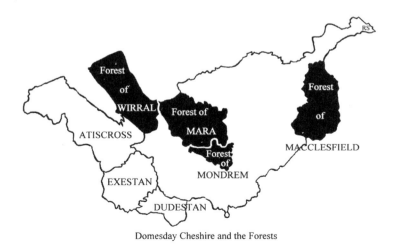

Domesday Cheshire and the Forests

card, but this one was significantly larger than the standard size. The buildings inside the wall were more imposing than those of other forts, while outside the wall, they erected an amphitheatre grand enough to keep a large population entertained. London's Royal Albert Hall can accommodate 5,272 people, but in this arena 8,000 or more could sit and watch gladiatorial combat while munching on fast food. It's true – archaeologists have dug up part of a gladiator's sword and discarded chicken bones! The amphitheatre, too, is the biggest yet found in Britain.

Why such overblown dimensions? No one knows for sure, but a look at the map gives us a possible clue. If you were an invader planning to conquer the entire British Isles and create a new province, where would you place the capital? A centrally-positioned port would be ideal; where better than Chester? Some historians have dared to suggest that the Romans intended Dewa to be the capital of Britannia. Had it retained that status, Britain, with a centralized capital, would have developed very differently.

The Angles, when they began to settle the region in the seventh century, probably found the old fort in ruins. It was absorbed into the great midland kingdom of Mercia, forming its insecure, underpopulated north-west corner, always neurotic about invasion by the Northumbrians or the Welsh. The name Mercia means boundary people, after all. In the late ninth century, this area found itself sitting on a new and more dangerous boundary; that between the English and the Danes. King Alfred and his son Edward the Elder eventually swept the invaders out of west Mercia and introduced the West Saxon shire system to the region. The once-proud kingdom was cut up (or 'sheared') into shires, each governed, on behalf of the king, by a sheriff. Legeceasterscir ('shire of the city of legions') was first drawn onto the map around AD 920. In time, when the legionary connection had been forgotten, the name was shortened to 'Cestrescir' and later slurred into 'Cheshire'.

The Normans became acquainted with the county in 1069, when they came to quell a serious rebellion. Their punishment was brutal and unforgettable: everywhere, dwellings were destroyed (200 in Chester alone), crops burned and people made destitute. A fertile land was turned into a desolate one. To rub it in, two-fifths of the county was afforested; in the great forests of Wirral, Mara, Mondrem and Macclesfield, the welfare of deer came before that of human beings.

In the Domesday Book (1086), Cheshire's western frontier was not the Dee, as today, but the river Clwyd. For over 500 years, between the reigns of King Offa of Mercia and King Edward I, a great slice of land that now belongs to Flintshire and the county of Wrexham, was in England. And what about that wiggly tail of land on the north-east that appears to have been added on as an afterthought? Why did Cheshire need an appendix of desolate moorland reaching out to the Yorkshire border? That is Longdendale, which had a good road across the Pennines. It may have been added at the insistence of mid-Cheshire salt traders who needed a direct route to Yorkshire, avoiding the tolls that were charged when crossing a county line.

The county's boundary saw little further change for 700 years. Its position on the Welsh border ensured that its people – largely Britons by blood but English in language and culture – were not destined for a peaceful history. On the contrary, they would win military glory both at home and abroad that would make them, of all people in England, 'midst proudest, proud'.

THE EARLS OF CHESTER

Having brought the English to heel, the Normans now turned their attention to the Welsh. The towns of Hereford and Shrewsbury had already been made into Marcher Earldoms (military buffer

Ranulph de Blondeville

zones that dominated the Welsh border), and Chester now became the third. Successive Earls of Chester were given the task of holding the line against Welsh intrusion, but most of them also took part in military campaigns all over England and across the Channel, usually, but not always, in the service of the king. The Earls held Cheshire and North Wales in an iron grip for 167 years.

At the entrance to Grosvenor Park, Chester, there is a pretty, half-timbered lodge (designed by John Douglas in 1866) whose gables are adorned with carvings of William I and seven of the Earls. They are dressed in chainmail with tunics of red, blue or gold, crowns on their heads and swords in their hands (some now broken or lost). Their coats of arms are shown beneath their feet.

What benign-looking chaps they are! Starting at the far left, we find King William, who has evidently usurped the place of the first Earl, Gerbod the Fleming. Gerbod, who may well have been in the fight at Hastings, was thrown into the job in 1070, and he had his hands full, controlling both the English and the Welsh. He soon gave it up and sailed off to France, where he was captured in battle and imprisoned, leaving the Earldom vacant.

To the right of William, in a blue frock emblazoned with a wolf's head, is Gerbod's replacement, Hugh d'Avranches, another possible Hastings veteran. Born in the small town of Avranches in Normandy, he ruled in Chester for thirty years, and subdued North Wales with such merciless efficiency that he became known as Hugh Lupus (Hugh the Wolf). In middle age, he enjoyed the good things in life, siring many illegitimate children and developing his waistline to such an extent that he could barely walk. When his final illness set in, he decided to repent his sins and become a monk. Four days later, he died, and is buried in Chester Cathedral, under the floor of the Chapter House. Not a nice man.

Next along, with no beard, wearing a little red number, again emblazoned with a wolf's head, is Hugh's son Richard d'Avranches. Why no beard? Because he was a teenager when he became Earl. At the age of 26, he lost his life in the *White Ship* disaster of 1120, and as there was no issue, the title passed to his cousin Ranulph le Meschine ('the Younger') the following year. During the interim, Welsh forces swarmed across Cheshire, killing, looting and burning down castles.

Furthest right, looking gorgeous in gold, is Ranulph himself, who held the title for nine years. Cheshire was, at this time, one of the most impoverished counties in England, so as compensation, other estates, scattered all over England and Wales, were added to the Earl's possessions. No surprise, then, that Ranulph, one of the most powerful magnates in England, spent little time in the county.

Turning to the east-facing gable, we meet his son, Ranulph de Gernon, who was Earl for twenty-five years, during which time England was torn apart by civil war. The Earl, fearful of losing some of his northern estates, rose in arms against King Stephen, then changed his mind and swore fealty to him, then rebelled again. He died in great agony, aged 54, when his host served him poison. And he looks so cute up there.

Ranulph's son Hugh de Kevelioc was the first Earl to be born on this side of the Channel – in Wales, as his name suggests.

Like his father, he could be wayward in his loyalties. He joined a revolt against King Henry II and was captured and imprisoned, but within a few years his estates had been restored to him and he was happy to fight for the king in Ireland.

Hugh's son, Ranulph de Blondeville, also born in Wales, succeeded him at the age of 11 and held the Earldom for over half a century. Unlike his two predecessors, he had the good sense to remain in the king's favour and went on to become one of the greatest barons in England. He witnessed the signing of the Magna Carta and, since Chester was a Marcher Earldom, not covered by the document, he drew up a Magna Carta of Chester to appease his own barons. Small in stature, he nevertheless distinguished himself in battle at home and abroad, went on the fifth crusade (1218–20) and built Beeston Castle. Thanks to his dashing reputation and romantic name, he has often featured in novels set in the reigns of King Richard I and King John.

Notice, below the figurine, Ranulph's coat of arms: three golden wheatsheaves on a blue ground; add a sword and we have the modern coat of arms of Cheshire. Wheatsheaves! Not the most appropriate symbol for such a pastoral county!

Furthest to the right is the last Earl, Ranulph's nephew John the Scot, son of Prince David of Scotland. He married the daughter of Llywelyn the Great, but died in 1237 at the age of 30, leaving no heir. He had four sisters, but King Henry III quickly stepped in and grabbed the Earldom for himself, 'lest so fair a dominion should be divided among women'. He gave it all to his son Edward, and, after 1254, 'Earl of Chester' became a title given to the heir to the throne. Prince Charles was created Earl of Chester when he was 9 years old.

The Cheshire motto, *Jure et Dignitate Gladii*, means 'By the law and dignity of the sword'.

THE COUNTY PALATINE

The Normans introduced the concept of the County Palatine to England, whereby a powerful Earl swore allegiance to the king but was allowed to rule the county independently of him. Cheshire was chosen for this honour because of its position on the Welsh border; it was to act as a barrier against insurgence, governed almost, but not quite, as a separate realm, independent from England.

The county managed its own affairs with a parliament made up of its own barons and was not represented at Westminster until 1543. In those heady, autonomous days it was not considered strange to use a phrase such as, 'He left Chester and returned to England.'

Regular fighting began to change the character of Cheshire men and blacken their reputation. A monk of St Albans wrote:

Because of their fickleness the people of those parts are more ready and accustomed to doing such things, because of former wars and local disputes they more readily resort to arms; and are more difficult to control than other people.

In 1400, 'the liege men of Shropshire' complained bitterly about gangs of Cheshire men who would misbehave in Shropshire and then nip back over the border to safety:

… for the said county is a County Palatine, and the inhabitants thereof cannot be punished in Cheshire for any crime or offence committed outside that county … even for High Treason.

To make matters worse, outlaws from England found haven here, adding their own criminal DNA to the mix. No wonder Cheshire developed a sense that it was different, independent, even privileged.

A few of these privileges lingered on for centuries until they were finally abolished in 1830. Even some weights and measure were different: the Cheshire acre covered 10,240 square yards, making it more than twice the size of an English acre. Until the nineteenth century, it was used by farmers all over Cheshire, while the statute acre meant nothing to them.

Inside the porch of Shotwick church (near the spot where a castle once controlled the Welsh border), there are deep grooves gouged into the stonework where archers used to sharpen their arrows.

WHEN CHESHIRE INVADED FRANCE

In the reign of Edward I, a good use was found for those pugnacious Cheshire men: they were transformed into elite troops. Criminals, even murderers, were promised a pardon if they signed up for 'service in the King's wars' – rather like rounding up all the football hooligans in England, giving them SAS training and quietly forgetting about their previous peccadillos. Already battle-hardened, they honed their skills even further in campaigns against the Scots and the French and came to be feared both at home and abroad.

In the mid-fourteenth century they were distinguished from other soldiers by their green and white livery – a short woollen coat coloured in two equal halves, à la Blackburn Rovers. All were strong enough to draw a 6ft bow of flexible yew or wych elm with a draw weight of over 100lb (more than twice that of the bows used today in the Olympics). Their arrows, with flights of swan, goose or even peacock feather, were of light ash with steel heads, able to penetrate chainmail and most kinds of plate armour at 250 yards.

It was the Hundred Years' War that forged their reputation. At the Battle of Sluys, in 1340, the archers fought on board ships, shooting twenty arrows per minute at the French vessels, while the enemy crossbows could manage only two bolts in return. Many French soldiers died on board their own ships before they could engage in battle.

At Crecy (1346) and Poitiers (1356), an eyewitness wrote: 'In the vanguard there were many knights and squires of Cheshire in the Prince's company and noble archers also.' Archers made up at least a third of the English army in both battles, and the storm of arrows they delivered drove the enemy into confusion, provoking them into desperate, ill-considered charges. Both battles were overwhelming victories for England – well, let's be honest, for Cheshire – over the French nobility. The shock waves were felt all over Europe.

As the demand for archers increased, each hundred in Cheshire turned itself into a soldier factory, churning out archers and men-at-arms as efficiently as the farms produced cheeses. Horses were needed too, and the county responded by breeding them; every Cheshire man of substance owned at least one stable of horses.

A succession of English kings turned to Cheshire in time of war, but our biggest royal fan was Richard II. In 1387, he awarded himself the title 'Prince of Chester', and, a few years later, began to shift his power base from London to Cheshire.

So useful were the Cheshire men that they were paid more than other soldiers and, when they finally hung up their bows, they were rewarded with goods and land. You could spot them by their dress. Cheshire knights and squires wore Richard's badge of a white hart on their shoulders. Records list many of their names, almost all of them evocative of Cheshire: William Donne de Kelsall, Peter de Legh, Adam Bostock, Richard de Cholmondeley, Ralph Davenport, Thomas de Beeston, etc. As for the rank and file archers, they wore the badge of a gilded crown. Richard selected a small band of them to be his bodyguard, charged with keeping watch over his bedchamber as he slept. In the event of a real threat to the king's person, a much larger force was ready to be called upon. In Parliament, when the king negotiated with his baronial rivals, these bully boys were there to see that he got his way. When Richard was finally deposed, one of the main charges against him was the behaviour of these tough, arrogant men, whose immunity from prosecution allowed them to rob, rape and murder as they wished.

In 1398, 'for the love he bore to the gentlemen and commons of the shire of Chester' the king raised the county's status from Palatinate to Principality, an honour that no other English county has ever received. The glory lasted only until the following year, when Henry Bolingbroke overthrew Richard, reversed his decision and punished the Cheshire men for their loyalty to him.

It was no surprise, then, that when Henry Percy (Harry Hotspur) hoisted the flag of rebellion, most of his army was recruited in Cheshire. The turmoil came to a crisis in 1403, in a field of peas near Shrewsbury – the first battle in which English archers fought one another on English soil. It was not a fair contest, of course: the king's archers were from England, but Percy's were from Cheshire. Jean de Waurin (later to witness the Battle of Agincourt) wrote: 'the sun lost its brightness so thick were the arrows', and, according to Thomas Walsingham, the king's men 'fell like leaves in autumn. Every one struck a mortal man.'

One arrow buried itself in the face of the king's son – later to be King Henry V. Suffering heavy losses, the entire right flank of the king's army turned and fled. The battle was as good as won – wasn't it? Hotspur, true to his name, decided to finish it quickly with a wild charge, but it's never a good idea to open your visor at a moment like that. He was killed, and after a period of confusion about which leader was dead, King Henry had the victory.

Having seen for himself the prowess of the Cheshire archers, Henry, naturally, recruited them for his own use, although it took time to win them over to the Lancastrian monarchy.

At the Battle of Agincourt in 1415, archers made up at least 80 per cent of the English force and, as ever, a disproportionate number were from Cheshire. Once again, the class system of warfare was turned on its head.

Back in the Palatinate, meanwhile, little had improved. Career soldiers, on returning home, found it hard to unlearn their violent ways, and the level of bow crime was still high.

Regarding warfare, more bad news was coming: the best armourers in Europe had been busy, creating breastplates that were lighter and stronger than ever. Arrows were no longer drilling holes through them; they were bouncing off. The bowmen were losing the arms race.

The Wars of the Roses brought division and misery to Cheshire. One of the first great battles was fought at Blore Heath (1459) just a few miles over the Staffordshire border. Many Cheshire men lined up in the Lancastrian ranks, wearing the badge of the swan that, at Queen Margaret's insistence, had been given 'to all the gentlemen of Cheshire'. However, a substantial number of their own kinsmen were staring back at them from the Yorkist position. Michael Drayton, in his *Poly-Olbion* (published in 1612), explained the tragedy that resulted:

> There Dutton Dutton kills: a Done doth kill a Done:
> A Booth a Booth: and Legh by Legh is overthrown:
> A Venables against a Venables doth stand:
> A Troutbeck fighteth with a Troutbeck hand to hand:
> There Molineaux doth make a Molineaux to die:
> Our Egerton the strength of Egerton doth try:
> O, Cheshire! Wert thou mad of thine own native gore,
> So much, until this day, thou never shedd'st before!
> Above two thousand men upon the earth were thrown,
> Of whom the greater part were naturally thine own.

Witnesses reckoned that more than half of the 3,000 dead on both sides were from Cheshire, making the result (a Yorkist victory) almost an irrelevance. Sir Thomas Fitton of Gawsworth, a loyal supporter of the House of Lancaster, had sixty-six tenants before the battle and afterwards only thirty-five. A traditional song that used to be sung all over the county, celebrating the triumphs of Cheshire bowmen, was never sung again.

Here is a curious footnote to the story of the Cheshire bowmen. The Shropshire writer H.E. Forrest, in his book *The Old Houses of Wenlock* (1915), found this entry in the church records:

1543 Feb 21.

Here was buried out of the almshouses John Trussingham, a
Cheshire man born, an aged lame man, for on Saturday before
departing he said to me, Sir Thomas Butler, Vicar of the Church
of the Holy Trinity of Much Wenlock, that he was of the age
of seven score years, and I said it could not be so, and he was,
as he had said, of the age of four score years at the battle of
Blower Heath, and since that, there were three score years (count
altogether, said he, and ye shall find seven score years, rather
more or less) …

King's Vale Royal (1656) makes a claim for the longevity
of Cheshire folk: 'The people there live till they be very old;
some are Grandfathers, their fathers still living; and some are
Grandfathers before they be married.'

But to take part in a battle at the age of eighty? On the
other hand, there is the case of Sir George Beeston of Bunbury,
who took part in the battle against the Spanish Armada in
1588 and was knighted for his heroism. According to the
historian George Ormerod, he was 102 when he died in 1601.
Work it out!

BRAVEHEART

It was Thursday, 4 September 1651, the day following the Battle
of Worcester. A straggling remnant of the Royalist force, having
been routed by the New Model Army, was returning home. The
soldiers were almost all Scotsmen, so they headed northward
until the road brought them to south Cheshire.

What they needed was a stop for food and rest before
continuing their journey. It was prudent to avoid Nantwich, a

Parliamentarian stronghold, so they headed for Sandbach, where they arrived at three o'clock in the afternoon. The little town was busy, enjoying a two-day September fair, quite unprepared for the arrival of a thousand armed cavalrymen. What happened next was reported in the weekly magazine *Mercurius Politicus*:

The enemy were then supposed to be about 1000 horse, and came through the town of Sanbatch that day, being the Fair-day: but the honest townsmen and countrymen perceiving their condition, fell upon them with clubs and staves, and the very poles wherewith they made their stalls and standings; and as they came down they still fell upon them, fetching some from off their horses. They so managed the business, that when the Scots offered to fire, they ran into their houses and as soon as that party was past which had the pistols and powder (there being only the frontiers that had shot) they fell still upon the remainder of the troops and continued pealing and billing them during the passage of all their horse. In this scuffle, the town took about one hundred of them and killed some; as also there were some of the countrymen killed. This relation is given by one who was an eye witness; it being very notable that such men should engage so great an armed body with such instruments. But the Lord had stricken a terror into the enemies' hearts who minded only the making good of their flight.

According to another report:

> The dispute was very hot for two or three hours, there were some townsmen hurt and two or three slain, the townsmen slew about nine or ten and took 100 prisoners, which I have sent to Chester, some of them officers and men of quality.

The Scots tried to get a night's sleep on a green about a mile away but were again attacked before dawn and fled with no more than a parting shot and a shout of defiance. On the following day, another disconsolate rabble passed through. The townsmen did battle again and took another fifty prisoners, again including officers, whom they locked up in the church.

The soldiers' horses had become so exhausted that many abandoned them and continued on foot, sleeping rough and foraging for food. Two local men, with the help of a sniffer dog, rounded up another sixteen of the stragglers and added them to the collection. A vicar, invited to preach at the church the following Sunday, wrote:

> The poor Scots were miserably used in the country, and so many of them put into the church at Sandbach that we could not preach in it; but I preached in the church-yard both ends of the day, to a great congregation.

Och, the shame of it! Had they simply been English Royalist soldiers, they might have passed through Sandbach unscathed, but these men were also foreigners. They should have heeded William Smith's description of Cheshire men, written a century earlier:

> They are of stomack, bold, and hardy; of stature, tall and mighty; withall impatient of wrong, and ready to resist the enemy or stranger, that shall invade their country. The very name whereof, they cannot abide, and namely, of a Scot.

The nineteenth-century researchers who collected Cheshire dialect words and tried to trace their origins were surprised to find that very few had been borrowed from the Welsh language. One of those few was the phrase 'dim sassnick', said of someone who pretends not to understand: 'It's aw dim sassnick with 'im.' Some Welsh people had a habit of replying to an unwelcome question with the words, 'dim Saesneg' ('no English'), whether they understood or not!

WELSHMEN OF EITHER SEX

1515. In this yeare was a fraye betwixte the cittizens of Chester and divers Waylshe men at St. Warburge Lane ende, but lytill hurte done for the Waylshe men fled.

Cheshire's ancient palatinate status led to an insularity so deep that it took centuries to fade. Until the late nineteenth century, visitors, whether from England or Wales, were lumped together as 'frem folk' – undesirable incomers. Some were fremmer than others, however, and the Welsh were the frem de la frem!

This attitude, naturally, was stronger in Chester than elsewhere in the county. The Welsh were the reason for Chester's existence; why else would you keep the walls in good repair, your arrows sharp and your eyes peeled? The Welsh never did manage to burn 'Caer' to the ground, but the suburb of Handbridge, lying on the unprotected side of the Dee, was not so lucky. In Wales they had another name for it: Treboeth, meaning 'burnt town'. According to one old story, the locals responded by building a wall of Welshmen's skulls near the river, as a sort of un-welcome mat.

Chester had another form of protection, apart from walls, the longbow and vigilance: the relics of St Werburgh, a Mercian princess who lived in the seventh century. She was canonised on the strength of miracles performed during her lifetime, such as bringing a dead (and eaten) goose back to life. After death, her bones were acquired by the monastery at Chester and preserved in a shrine, where they did a splendid job of protecting the city. When Gruffydd ap Llywelyn, the eleventh-century Welsh King, surrounded Chester with a mighty army, the defenders retaliated by displaying the casket that contained the saint's remains. When they saw it, the king and his men were 'smytten with blyndnes' and forced to retreat.

Richard d'Avranches, who, you will remember, was one of the Earls of Chester, went on a pilgrimage to the shrine of St Winefride at Holywell and was unexpectedly cornered and trapped by a Welsh force. His own troops could do nothing to help; they were stationed at the furthest tip of Wirral, and no ships were available to carry them across the estuary. In despair, the captains knelt and made a heartfelt supplication to St Werburgh. To their joy and astonishment, the waters parted before them like the Red Sea and the relieving force was able to march across to Holywell and rescue the beleaguered Earl.

The best-known example of Chester's real or supposed antipathy to the Welsh is a proclamation of 1403 that commanded the citizens of the city to keep a close eye on visitors from over the border. All modern Cestrians have heard of it and most take a delight in regaling Welsh visitors with their own garbled versions of it, usually involving longbows or crossbows shooting from the city walls at certain times of the day when there is an 'r' in the month. In fact, the text boils down to four instructions:

> We order that forthwith … you cause to be driven out of the walls of the city aforesaid all manner of Welshmen of either sex, male as well as female … and that no Welshman, or any person of Welsh extraction or sympathies … remain within the walls of the said city, nor enter into the same after sunset, under pain of cutting off his head …

There are two things to note here. Firstly, the aliens were allowed to hang around while the shops were open – Chester needed its tourists even in those days. Secondly, for all the brutality, 'Welshmen of either sex' implies an enlightened attitude to transgender issues.

… and that on no day whatsoever he journey or presume to go into the city with arms upon him … except for one little knife for carving his dinner.

That seems fair enough.

And that they enter into no wine or beer tavern in the same city …

An excellent law.

… and that they hold no meetings or assemblies in the same, and that three of the same Welshmen come not together within the walls aforesaid. Which thing, if they do, they shall be forthwith taken for rebels against the peace, and be committed to the gaol …

Another wise precaution – an assembly of Welshmen can so easily become a choir.

We command that you cause such guard to be ordered, set, and maintained at each gate of the city aforesaid, with watches upon the walls and elsewhere in the same city by night and day.

It all sounds like a clear case of Cestrian Cymrophobia, but in fact it is nothing of the kind. The ruling was issued, not by the Mayor of Chester, but by the 16-year-old Prince Henry (later to be crowned Henry V) who had fought in the Battle of Shrewsbury a few weeks earlier. You will recall from an earlier chapter that most Cheshire men fought against the king in that conflict – they flocked to the banner of Harry Hotspur, who had formed an alliance with the Welsh rebel Owain Glyndwr. The king, therefore, was having sleepless nights, worried that the Cheshire archers, the most feared fighting men in Europe, might stiffen the ranks of Glyndwr's army and march south. For that reason, he wanted no Anglo–Welsh fraternising or collusion in Chester.

By the nineteenth century, border warfare was just a folk memory, but when English and Welsh bumped into one another there were still minor scores to settle. George Borrow relates an interesting encounter in his book *Wild Wales* (1862):

Early the next morning I departed from Chester to Llangollen, distant about twenty miles; I passed over the noble bridge and proceeded along a broad and excellent road, leading in a direction almost due south through pleasant meadows. I felt very happy – and no wonder; the morning was beautiful, the birds sang merrily, and a sweet smell proceeded from the new-cut hay in the fields, and I was bound for Wales. I passed over the river Allan and through two villages called, as I was told, Pulford and Marford, and ascended a hill; from the top of this hill the view is very fine. To the east are the high lands of Cheshire, to the west the bold hills of Wales, and below, on all sides a fair variety of wood and water, green meads and arable fields.

'You may well look around, Measter,' said a Waggoner, who, coming from the direction in which I was bound, stopped to breathe his team on the top of the hill; 'You may well look around – there isn't such a place to see the country from, far and near, as where we stand. Many come to this place to look about them.'

I looked at the man, and thought I had never seen a more powerful-looking fellow; he was about six feet two inches high, immensely broad in the shoulders, and could hardly have weighed less than sixteen stone. I gave him the seal of the morning, and asked whether he was Welsh or English.

'English, Measter, English; born t'other side of Beeston, pure Cheshire, Measter.'

'I suppose,' said I, 'there are few Welshmen such big fellows as yourself.'

'No, Measter,' said the fellow, with a grin, 'there are very few Welshmen so big as I, or yourself either, they are small men mostly, Measter, them Welshers, very small men – and yet the fellows can use their hands. I am a bit of a fighter, Measter, at least I was before my wife made me join the Methodist connection, and I once fit with a Welshman at Wrexham, he came from the hills, and was a real Welshman, and shorter than myself by a whole head and shoulder, but he stood up against me, and gave me more than play for my money, till I gripped him, flung him down and myself upon him, and then of course 'twas all over with him.'

'You are a noble fellow,' said I, 'and a credit to Cheshire. Will you have sixpence to drink?'

'Thank you, Measter, I shall stop at Pulford, and shall be glad to drink your health in a jug of ale.'

I gave him sixpence, and descended the hill on one side, while he, with his team, descended it on the other.

'A genuine Saxon,' said I …

Nowadays, Welsh people can stroll down Marford Hill with no fear of such resistance. Between 2012 and 2015, 8,590 crossed the border unmolested and settled in Cheshire, helping to make the western half of the county the Welshest place in England. And which surname do you think is the commonest in Cheshire? No, not Smith, but Jones!

The clock on Chester Town Hall has only three faces. The fourth being blank. Any Cestrian will tell you why: 'That side faces Wales, and we won't give 'em the time o' day!'

FILLING THE TEAPOT

The old outline of Cheshire has been likened to a teapot, with its handle in the Pennines and its spout over to the west, forever pouring Darjeeling into the Irish Sea.

Between 1800 and 1900, its population more than quadrupled, filling from the top downwards as industrial towns sprang up in both the spout and the handle. Wages were higher there, but within a few generations, those who could afford to began to dream a dream, as if some ancestral memory was calling them back to the land. As Fletcher Moss of Didsbury put it in 1901:

> Therefore we also wish to breathe the pure fresh country air, to see the woodlands carpeted with acres of hyacinth blue, to listen to the lark's ecstatic hymn, and to smell 'the smell of the field which the Lord hath blessed.' Whither can we better go for all these pleasures than southwards, amid the old familiar scenes in Cheshire?

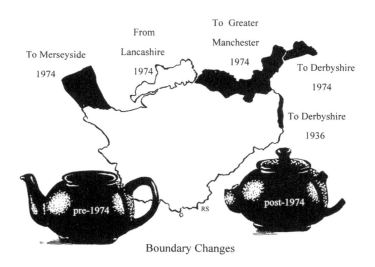

Boundary Changes

Those who found those pleasures eventually woke up to find themselves breathing a more suburban air, of course, but there was a bigger shock to come – 1974, the year of broken crockery! The spout and the handle were knocked off and donated to the new counties of Merseyside and Greater Manchester, so that the teapot now looked more like a casserole. There was a small consolation: the casserole was given a lid in the form of Warrington and Widnes, but the county was much reduced, both in area and population. Moreover, the boroughs of Warrington and Halton (including Widnes) became unitary authorities in 1998, so the lid is rattling a little.

It could have been even worse: in 1969, the government was planning to toss the whole teapot into the bin!

IS CHESHIRE IN T' NORTH?

Is Cheshire in the North, like Lancashire, or does it belong in the Midlands, like Staffordshire? Many would claim that the river Mersey (the name means 'boundary river') is the dividing line. It used to separate Mercia from Northumbria, but thanks to Anglo–Saxon belligerence, it was never a stable frontier. During the seventh century, the area we now call Cheshire was grabbed by Northumbria and snatched back by Mercia time and time again.

In the late medieval period, the County Palatine defined itself in opposition to Wales and didn't much care to which region of England it belonged.

However, in more recent centuries, and particularly after the Industrial Revolution, Cheshire and Lancashire have been bound together in a symbiotic relationship. The teeming manufacturing towns of Lancashire would have clemmed without their close agricultural neighbour supplying milk, cheese, potatoes and oats, while the farmers could not have provided them without the goods that were made in Lancashire. This is a wild over-simplification, since Cheshire has its own industrial towns in Cheshire and parts of north Lancashire are rural, but it is broadly true. The expansion of Manchester and Liverpool, both at the extreme south of Lancashire, has pulled the two counties even closer together.

We also speak in a very similar way. As long ago as 1817, Roger Wilbraham wrote, in the introduction to his book *An Attempt at a Glossary of Some Words Used in Cheshire*:

> The very great resemblance of the dialects of Cheshire and of Lancashire may be observed by the frequent repetition of the abbreviation Lan. in this Glossary.

Even further back in history, the Elizabethan poet Michael Drayton wrote:

> Thy natural sister shire; and linked unto thee so,
> That Lancashire along with Cheshire still doth go.

So where, exactly, does the north begin? Stuart Maconie, in his book *Pies and Prejudice: In Search of the North*, makes a case for Crewe as not only the gateway to, but also the beginning of the north. One criterion is the use of affectionate terms to strangers: within twenty minutes of arriving in the town, he had been 'loved' by several women of a certain age, and 'petted', 'lover-ed' and 'luvvie'd' by several more (I must go to Crewe more often).

If you are still unsure, I suggest that you simply ask a few natives. They all give the same answer!

HAS CHESHIRE ALWAYS BEEN WELL-OFF?

Many visitors have asked me this loaded question!

Always? Since the first hunter-gatherers colonised the region following the last Ice Age? We have seen that, for much of the Middle Ages, Cheshire was the crime capital of England, and certainly one of its poorest counties.

The lowest ebb came during the aftermath of the Civil War, when Cheshire was gripped by plague and starvation and grass grew high in the streets of Chester. In 1647, Parliament issued an order that urged the south-eastern counties of England to have a whip-round to help Cheshire people, who 'if they be not presently relieved in an extraordinary way, are like to perish for want, and to endanger the infecting [of] the adjacent counties'.

But what about the Victorian era: didn't Cheshire grow fat through efficient, intensive agriculture?

Not according to the agricultural surveys of the day. In 1850, they found that about 900 farms in the county had less than 10 acres! Many of the older farmhouses on the plain were little wattle-and-daub buildings, some no more than 6ft high at the eaves, and without a privy. In Wirral and the west, wooden ploughs were still used, fields were not properly drained and seeds were still scattered by hand. Samuel Bagshaw (1850) wrote:

> On the whole, Cheshire is inferior to many counties in agriculture. It wants, however, only the application of capital and the superintendence of men of true practical science to become one of the finest agricultural counties in England.

Those words were heeded, of course; Cheshire farmers pulled their socks up, but I think we have buried the notion that Cheshire was *always* well-off.

A fairer question would be: is Cheshire well-off today?

Almost anyone, whether they have visited the county or not, will answer 'Yes'. They may express it smugly:

> Our affluent readers are keen to know about the best of fashion, interiors, motoring, antiques, education, hotels and restaurants. (*Cheshire Life Magazine*)

hypocritically:

> It's like England, only there's no class system, just the haves and the haves-even-more. (Jeremy Clarkson – not exactly a 'have-not')

or sneeringly:

> It is easy to mock Cheshire, but then that's hardly a reason not to. Cheshire is mock everything: mock gentility, mock Tudor Georgian, mock family, mock style, mock casual and mock happiness. (The late A.A. Gill)

So, how many of these 'haves and haves-even-mores' does Cheshire have? A 2014 report on Britain's HNWIs (High Net Worth Individuals) by New World Wealth found that 17,600 of them live in Cheshire, placing the county a modest 15th in the league table. Surrey, with a population only slightly larger than Cheshire's, has a whopping 59,800, which shows the absurdity of calling Cheshire 'the Surrey of the North'.

Alderley Edge, admittedly, is home to about 700 of these HNWIs, but nine southern towns of similar size can beat that, and Windsor, with 1,300, makes it look quite humble.

But what about all those rich footballers?

Yes, isn't Cheshire a county 'besmirched by footballers', as Jonathan Meades once sniffed? Well, let us suppose that every single one of the 600–700 Premiership footballers decided to commute from Cheshire to their daily training in London, Newcastle or wherever; in that case, one in every 1,600 Cheshire people would be a footballer – not enough to do much serious besmirching.

But it's an expensive place to live, isn't it?

In 2015, the average price of a house in Cheshire was £232,000, placing it 27th in the league table of counties; a little below halfway. No, Cheshire is not an expensive place to live.

But isn't there a 'Golden Triangle' that has the biggest concentration of millionaires, or something?

Indeed there is. Turn to the map at the beginning of this book and draw a line from Prestbury to Alderley Edge, then up to Wilmslow, and from there back to Prestbury. When Cheshire is mentioned in the media, it is usually to this part, and this part alone, that they refer.

Now compare that triangle with the whole county. What a minuscule area! Paint the rest blue and it looks like the sail of a tiny yacht, lost on the vast ocean of Cheshire. Nor is it the only sail on the horizon: Yorkshire has a Golden Triangle, many times the size of Cheshire's, reaching out from Leeds to York and Harrogate, while Birmingham's stretches all the way from Solihull to Rugby and Oxford.

But Cheshire's a Tory stronghold, surely?

Again, everybody seems to think so:

Cheshire votes Tory to a large extent and defiantly so, even when the candidate is Neil Hamilton. (Stuart Maconie, 2007)

Cheshire is divided into eleven parliamentary constituencies. In the 2017 General Election, seven of them (City of Chester, Crewe and Nantwich, Ellesmere Port and Neston, Halton, Warrington North, Warrington South, and Weaver Vale) were won by Labour, while the other four (Congleton, Eddisbury,

Macclesfield and Tatton) went to the Conservatives. In total, 278,044 voted Labour while 263,922 voted Conservative.

Local government follows a similar pattern: Cheshire is divided into four districts, three of which are Labour-controlled. So, Cheshire, unusually for a Tory stronghold, tends to vote Labour.

The question arises: if all of the above is true (it is), how did such a modest county become a target for so much vitriolic nonsense? I suggest that we are dealing with that chronic British ailment, class-neurosis. Compare the sniping of Gill and Clarkson with the view of a relative outsider, Bill Bryson, who visited Alderley Edge in his book *The Road to Little Dribbling* (2015):

> I was delighted to find that Alderley Edge is a very attractive place, with a handsome, well-maintained high street … I thought it would be like Beverley Hills, filled with overwrought houses with big walls and automated gates, but there wasn't much of that at all. Most of the houses were big, but not ostentatious, and on the whole seemed reasonably restrained and tasteful. In a strange way, it was disappointing and comforting at the same time.

Bryson, you see, is a sensible American; no one, in his native Iowa, feels guilty about moving up in the world and, therefore, has no need look for a scapegoat.

Attractive? Certainly. Ostentatious? Not particularly. Cheshire is a remarkable county in many ways, but not in that way. I hope the reader is comforted, and not too disappointed!

Chester comedian Russ Abbot was voted the funniest man on television five times, but his childhood was not so glamorous; he and his five brothers grew up in dire poverty: 'My Mum used to sew rubber pockets in our trousers so we could steal soup.'

2

ROMANCE

WIRRALIANS

Wirral place names have a curious sound, different from those we find on the Cheshire Plain: Noctorum and Liscard, for example, are both of Irish origin. Landican is Welsh – spell it with a double 'L' and its origin becomes obvious. Others, like Thingwall, Heswall, Thurstaston and Meols, derive from Old Norse, even if the people who named them had come over from Dublin. The same goes for all the names that end in '-by': West Kirby, Raby, Irby, Pensby, Frankby, Whitby and so on. And Wallasey? No, that's an English name, but it means 'Island of the Foreigners!' Yes, the people of this peninsula are a mixed-up lot; not so much Wirralians as 'We're Aliens'.

Surrounded on three sides by the sea, they were always semi-detached from the rest of Cheshire, developing into a sturdy, independent breed with a reputation for bolshiness. In the fourteenth century, Edward the Black Prince found it to be the one part of Cheshire where it was difficult to recruit soldiers for the war in France.

The poem 'Sir Gawain and the Green Knight', written around the same time, tells us:

In the wyldrenesse of Wyrale – wonde ther bot lyte,
That auther God other gome wyth goud hert lovied …

(In the wilderness of Wirral – few lived there who were loved by God or good-hearted men.)

A damning view; let's see if it is justified …

WRECKERS AND SMUGGLERS

Wallasey for wreckers, Poulton for trees,
Liscard for honest men and Seacombe for thieves.

(Wirral saying)

Much of Wirral remained a 'wyldrenesse' even until the early nineteenth century. Here, for example, is historian George Ormerod's 1819 description of Oxton (whose grand Victorian houses now form a conservation area):

> The village of Oxton is mean and small, composed of wretched, straggling huts, amongst roads only not impassable. The township occupies an eminence which commands a full view of the buildings and shipping of Liverpool, exhibiting a picture resembling metropolitan bustle and splendour almost immediately below the eye; but no degree of civilization or improvement has reached this part of the opposite shore, which is a scene of solitude broken in upon only with the voice of the cowherd or the cry of the plover. Bleak and barren moors stretch round it in every direction, and exhibit an unmixed scene of poverty and desolation.

To be fair, Ormerod wasn't a huge fan of Wirral in general, as these descriptions show:

Overpool – 'a few ragged huts and a farm house'.

Neston – 'naked and cheerless'.

Stoak – 'the village is a collection of rugged and filthy hovels scattered around the church.'

Picton – 'in roads, appearance and in inhabitants it may be safely said to present a complete picture of barbarism.'

No wonder, then, that Wirral people were driven to find shady methods of supplementing their meagre incomes. One such was 'wrecking': the practice of looting wrecked cargo ships and robbing the sailors, both living and dead. There is little evidence that ships were, or could have been, deliberately enticed towards disaster by wreckers, but as soon as one did hit the rocks they were ready. They would spread frightening rumours among the credulous locals: ghosts had been seen on the beach, or cannibals were hiding in caves, ready to pounce on passers-by – anything to keep the beach clear so that they could work undisturbed.

In 1839 a report on wrecking found:

Cheshire and Cornwall are the worst. On the Cheshire coast not far from Liverpool, they will rob those who have escaped the perils of the sea and come safe on shore, and mutilate dead bodies for the sake of rings and ornaments.

According to James Stonehouse (1863):

On stormy days and nights, crowds might have been seen hurrying to the shore with carts, barrows, horses, asses, or oxen even, which were made to draw timber, bales, boxes or anything that the raging waters might have cast up. Many a half-drowned sailor has had a knock on the sconce whilst trying to obtain a footing that has sent him reeling back into the seething water, and many a house had been suddenly replenished with eatables

and drinkables and furniture and garniture, where previously
bare walls and wretched accommodation only were visible.

Hilbre Island was perfectly positioned for these activities. It
provided a haven for fishing boats, and, until the 1840s, there
was a pub on the island. Richard Ayton visited in 1813:

> A man and his wife are the only permanent inhabitants, and
> they are said by various arts of industry to have amassed great
> wealth, not less, fame has ventured to assert, than a thousand
> pounds. The crews of some small vessels which find a harbour
> under one side of the island, are the great customers of their tap-
> room, but their riches have been gained principally by wrecking,
> for which business their situation here is said to be admirably
> calculated. She was an active partner in the miscellaneous
> business of her husband, having hardihood enough to despise
> the privileges of her petticoats.

Other Wirralians made a living by smuggling. As the river Dee
gradually silted up, boats heading for Chester were obliged to
find a mooring further along the coast and transport their goods
to the port by road. This made the smuggler's job much easier: in
stormy weather a ship might drop its anchor almost anywhere
between Parkgate and Hoylake and the small band of customs
officers could not be everywhere at once; besides, it was not
unknown for customs men to indulge in the practice themselves!

An operation was announced by the use of a password, such
as 'the ghost walks tonight'. Then, just like the wreckers, they
would put around the ghost stories: the black dog of Heswall
Beacons was abroad again, or the headless dog of Whitfield
Common, or the green ghost of Heswall Dales, or the Devil's
black hearse had again been seen rattling along the road between
Gayton and the beach. If the job was on Heswall Shore they

would retell the story of two smugglers who had finished a quarrel by stabbing one another to death and whose spirits still haunted the tideline.

At nightfall, ordinary, respectable tradesmen were transformed into furtive but well-armed smugglers. As the ghost-fearing folk lay abed, goods were quietly loaded into small boats to be rowed ashore and dropped on some quiet beach, well away from the bright lights of Parkgate. The people of the villages were largely inter-related and greeted outsiders with an impenetrable wall of silence.

At Heswall, a purpose-built cave was carved out of the rock as a depot for contraband.

Goods were often seized, of course, in which case they would be taken to the custom houses of Parkgate or Chester and sold at auctions that were advertised in the papers: hundreds of yards of Irish linen, gallon after gallon of whisky, rum, brandy, gin and wine, boxes of tea and coffee, boxes of tobacco ...

Or it might simply vanish like the morning dew. The customs officers were only human, after all.

MOTHER REDCAP

During the late eighteenth and early nineteenth centuries, the smugglers of Wirral had their own headquarters: a pub on the Mersey shore near Egremont. If you know the area, you must dismiss the present suburban reality from your mind and imagine Ormerod's 'bleak and barren moors' stretching as far as the eye can see. Now picture a small house almost at the water's edge, an old building dating from the end of the sixteenth century, with walls 3ft thick. No road led to the building, so the only convenient way to call by was by boat – a real seaman's tavern. It was known to all as Mother Redcap's, because the landlady – 'a comely, fresh-coloured, Cheshire-spoken woman' – always wore a red cap.

It had a weathervane whose purpose was to warn smugglers not of wind direction but whether or not the customs men had got wind of their plans. When it was pointing to the house the coast was clear, if pointing seaward, beware!

The house had extensive cellars and a network of tunnels where contraband could be stored. At times, large amounts of money were also kept down there, because seamen on the privateers were happy to trust Mother Redcap with their pay. After her death, there were, inevitably, rumours of fortunes buried somewhere in the cellars but none were ever found. In time of war, when press gangs were looking for merchant sailors to man the ships, the same cellars served as hiding places.

The front door was made of oak, 5in thick, studded and barred on the inside and strong enough to keep most intruders out. If anyone did succeed in forcing it open, a trapdoor was triggered and the trespasser fell through to the cellar 8ft below.

Today, a nursing home stands on the spot, but it bears the name Mother Redcap's, so the lady is not quite forgotten.

GOBBINS OR WOOLLYBACKS?

Strangely enough, the nickname that people in the rest of Cheshire used for Wirralians doesn't reflect these lawless habits at all: they called them 'gobbins', and their peninsula 'Gobbinshire'. A gobbin is the same as a gawfin, gawbie, gawm, gob or goufe – all Cheshire words for 'fool' and we haven't even moved beyond the letter 'G'. The people of Wirral were dismissed as halfwits; half-man half-biscuit, you might say.

That thinly spread, rural population was soon to be outnumbered by newcomers from over the river, and they were given a new name by their Liverpool cousins: 'woollybacks'. Is either name fair? No, the list of famous and talented Wirralians is far too long for that!

*   *

Which mountaineer was the first to conquer Mount Everest? In 1924, Birkenhead's Sandy Irvine and Mobberley's George Mallory climbed to within 800ft of the summit; then, after a sudden snow squall, they were 'lost to sight between earth and heaven'. In 1999, the eerily well-preserved body of Mallory was found at 27,000ft, but no one can say for certain whether he reached the top or not. When asked why on earth he wanted to climb to the top of Everest, Mallory gave the famous reply: 'Because it's there.'

HILDEBURGH'S EYE

In the utmost brinke of this Promontorie lieth a small hungrie barren and sandie isle, called Il-bre which had sometime a little cell of monkes in it. (William Camden, *c*.1586)

The coastline of Cheshire, if we exclude the estuaries of the Mersey and the Dee, is less than 8 miles long, so it comes as a surprise to many that three tidal islands belong to the county: Hilbre Island, Middle Eye (only a quarter of Hilbre's size), and the diminutive Little Eye. Small islands, admittedly, but the two larger ones both have sheer cliff faces that rise to 56ft. Geologists visit the islands to study the complex layering in the sandstone; botanists come looking for plants such as rock sea lavender (*Limonium binervosum*) and sea spleenwort (*Asplenium marinum*), which are found nowhere else in Cheshire; birdwatchers are attracted by the great flocks of wading birds: knot, dunlin, oystercatcher, in their tens of thousands. Day-trippers come for the sheer exhilaration of the place and the chance to see grey seals and porpoises. If you have not yet visited, put it on your list, but heed the words of John Leland (*c*.1540):

> This Hillebyri at the floode is al environed with water as an isle, and then the trajectus [crossing] is a quarter of a mile over, and 4 fadome depe of water, and at ebbe a man may go over the sand.

In Leland's time, Hilbre was a busier place. There is even a record, during Elizabeth I's reign, of no fewer than 4,000 foot soldiers and 200 horse troops camping on the island en route for Ireland – an astonishing mental picture until you realise that

Hilbre has dwindled in size since that era. Maps of the time show just one squarish island, nearly a mile long. Even so, it was not a fun place to hang around in. In 1565, Sir Henry Sidney (father of the more famous Sir Philip) was marooned on Hilbre for days while his ship waited for a favourable wind and wrote in a letter: 'I was never so wery of a place, for here is nother meat, drynk nor any good lodging.'

When the Spanish Armada threatened England, there was even talk of fortifying the island, to prevent the enemy from blockading the port of Chester, and from August 1940 to May 1941, when German bombers were paying regular nocturnal visits to Liverpool, fires were lit on Hilbre in an attempt to mislead the pilots.

It was all much more peaceful in the late eleventh century when the Benedictine monks of Chester came to Hildeburgh's Eye and set up a small monastic community with a church and a shrine dedicated to the Virgin Mary. Thither, according to Raphael Holinshed, went 'a sort of superstitious fools, in pilgrimage to our Lady of Hilbre by whose offerings the monks there were cherished and maintained'.

In 1852, a sandstone cross was dug up on the island, dating from about AD 1000, but no other traces of the monks' presence have been found; nor has any historian identified Hildeburgh with any certainty. Was she an Anglo–Saxon saint? Did she live on the island? Whoever she was, her island was a destination for those 'superstitious fools' until the dissolution of the monasteries, after which a couple of monks were allowed to stay there for a few years, but only to maintain a beacon for shipping.

On the seaward side of the main island there is a cave, long known as The Lady's Cave, and, inside it, a flat ledge of natural sandstone that is called The Lady's Shelf. This sets the scene for one of the old tales of Hilbre, in the time when just one young monk lived on the island.

THE LADY'S CAVE

It was late afternoon, the tide was coming in fast, and the monk, knowing that the sea would soon wrap itself around his island, decided to go down to the beach while he still had the chance. The wind had been blowing relentlessly all day, tossing shells and scraps of seaweed all over the island, but he needed driftwood for his fire, so he wrapped up warmly and ventured out to face the storm.

The waves were lashing higher and higher. 'Lord, have mercy on any poor souls who are out at sea today and bring them home safely,' he said out loud.

He happened to pass a large cave that he had often explored in the past. Today, though, there was something unexpected: on a shelf of rock inside the cave a body lay stretched out. A drowned seaman, perhaps? The monk hurried over, pulled away the rubbery sea-wrack that had tangled itself around the body and found, not a sailor but a young woman. Her face was deathly white, her body chilled, but she was still breathing faintly. Quickly, he lifted her up and carried her up the worn sandstone steps to his cell, where he sat her down before a little fire and draped his thickest blanket around her shoulders.

She could not, he thought, be a local peasant girl, for her robe was of the finest cloth and adorned with a jewelled brooch. After a few minutes, she opened her blue eyes and looked at her surroundings in surprise. The monk poured out a small bowl of pottage and placed it in front of her, but she would not pick it up. She was too exhausted to move – almost too exhausted to speak – but with a little coaxing, he persuaded her to tell her story.

'My father is an important man, the Lord of Shotwick Castle. He's a proud man too. He wanted the best for his daughter. He chose a wealthy husband for me, a high-born Welsh knight. I was to become a lady of high degree. But ah!'

She paused and looked into his eyes.

'I was already in love! A young squire in my father's service. What was I to do? Father flew into a rage when I told him! He locked me up in my chamber. He shouted at me from behind the door, threatening me, saying he would send me to a nunnery if I disobeyed him. He would disinherit me and leave me a beggar. He told me that he had already sent my darling away and I would never see him again!'

She closed her eyes for a few moments, as if to recover a little strength before continuing.

'In time, though, his anger died down. A few days ago, he released me and begged me to forgive him for his unkindness. To make it up to me, he took me on a sailing trip; he knows I love nothing better than to be out at sea. The sun was shining, the sea was blue, I stood at the prow to feel the wind in my hair. Then the weather changed. In the blink of an eye, that gentle wind blew up into a raging gale, rain lashed down on us and our poor little boat … I went below deck and found that father's mood had changed just as quickly. Now there was a storm in his eyes. He thrust a letter into my hands and ordered me to read it. The letter said that my true love had been thrown from his horse – he was dead!'

Tears had begun to trickle down the lady's cheeks.

'I couldn't bear it. I went up on deck again, and – I hardly knew what I was doing – climbed onto the ship's bulwarks and threw myself into the sea. The shock of the cold water almost killed me. Then I looked back at the ship. Father was leaning over the side, calling to me! He was horrified, all his anger abated. It had been a trick, he shouted, the letter was only a forgery. My love was alive and well and I was free to marry him if I wished. A rope was thrown out to me. All I had to do was take hold of it and they would haul me aboard. I could see the rope floating on the surface, but the wind was blowing the boat away from me, carrying it out of reach. I drifted, drifted, further and further away. After that, I remember nothing.'

'Until I found you!' said the monk. She smiled and closed her eyes.

'Don't worry,' he added, reassuringly, 'I shall write to the abbot at Chester and he will send word to your …'

But the lady, drained by the effort of telling her story, had fallen asleep. The monk banked up the fire and retired to his bed.

Next morning, he found her sitting as he had left her, the cold pottage untouched, but her spirit had departed during the night. He buried her on the island, lining her grave with flowers of samphire, sea lavender and a sprig or rosemary from his herb garden.

The monk's cell has long since crumbled away, but the Lady's Cave and the flat ledge where she lay are just as they were, all those centuries ago.

ACROSS THE SANDS OF DEE

Charles Kingsley's story *The Water Babies* made him famous throughout the English-speaking world, but he also wrote poems, of which 'The Sands of Dee' is one of the best-remembered.

Kingsley conceived his poem at a social gathering where he eavesdropped on the conversation of two gentlemen as they admired a painting on the wall. It was by the landscape painter Copley Fielding; a depiction of the desolate, tidal wilderness at the mouth of the Dee estuary. Evening was coming on, a grey shroud of rain was approaching from the Welsh side, and cattle were coming home, plodding wearily through pools and creeks. One of the men remarked that it reminded him of a touching story he once heard of a young girl who, while fetching cattle home across the sands, was cut off and stranded as the tide rushed in. Her drowned body was discovered the following day.

As they talked, a young lady (with whom Kingsley may, or
may not, have been in love), played a haunting, melancholy
tune on the piano. The combination of those three elements: the
atmospheric painting, the old, sad tale and the plaintive melody,
ignited his imagination and produced this poem:

'O Mary, go and call the cattle home,
And call the cattle home,
And call the cattle home,
Across the sands of Dee.'
The western wind was wild and dark with foam,
And all alone went she.

The western tide crept up along the sand,
And o'er and o'er the sand,
And round and round the sand,
As far as eye could see.
The rolling mist came down and hid the land:
And never home came she.

'O, is it weed, or fish, or floating hair –
A tress of golden hair,
A drowned maiden's hair,
Above the nets at sea?'
Was never salmon yet that shone so fair
Among the stakes of Dee.

They row'd her in across the rolling foam,
The cruel crawling foam,
The cruel hungry foam,
To her grave beside the sea.
But still the boatmen hear her call the cattle home,
Across the sands of Dee.

Charles Kingsley was a canon of Chester Cathedral between 1870 and 1873. During that time, he founded the Chester Society for Natural Science, Literature and Art, which later led to the foundation of the Grosvenor Museum.

THE CHAUCER OF CHESHIRE

In the British Library there is a manuscript dating from about 1400 that contains four poems: 'Pearl', 'Cleanness', 'Patience' and 'Sir Gawain and the Green Knight'. They were composed only a few years before Chaucer began *The Canterbury Tales*, yet they come from a literary tradition that was alien to him. They are written in an alliterative format that was popular in the north and west of England, where French poetry had exerted less influence. The poems make it clear that their author was a well-educated man of high rank, although he probably had not visited London or moved in courtly circles. If he had not been to university he nevertheless understood Latin and French, had a deep understanding of theology, and was familiar with French romances. He also shows great practical knowledge of subjects such as heraldry, hunting and banquets. He was a poet of genius, but since he did not sign his work, we can only call him 'the Gawain Poet'.

If you find *The Canterbury Tales* tough to understand, be prepared for even slower progress here: these poems are written in the dialect of the north-west Midlands, almost certainly somewhere in the eastern half of Cheshire. Chaucer himself would have had trouble understanding it, so try a modern translation before tackling the original!

Apart from the dialect, there are two other indications of Cheshire origin. Firstly, some historians have tentatively identified the poet as a Cheshire gentleman named John Massey.

Secondly, in 'Sir Gawain and the Green Knight', although his geography is vague, he makes special mention of Wirral, with some disparaging observations about its people.

These poems are written in alliterative verse, the form used by the Beowulf poet (another nameless genius) many centuries earlier. Instead of rhyme we have the repetition of an initial consonant or vowel within each line. An example from 'Gawain':

> If ye wyl lysten this laye bot on littel quile,
> I schal telle hit astit, as I in toun herde,
> with tonge;
> As hit is stad and stoken
> In stori stif and stronge,
> With lel letteres loken,
> In londe so has ben longe.

In modern English: 'If you will listen to this lay a little while, I shall tell it, as I heard it told in the town, as it is set down in writing, in verses stiff and strong, with letters well linked, as it has long been in our land.'

All four poems follow a very strict and complex scheme of alliteration, metre and verse structure that requires considerable skill. That is why, in *The Canterbury Tales*, the Parson introduces his tale with an apology for using mere prose:

> But trust well, I am a Southern man;
> I can't speak rum ram ruf by letter …

In 'Pearl', the poet mourns the loss of a precious pearl in a garden. The reader, after first taking it literally, slowly realises that he is actually speaking about the recent death of his daughter, Marguerite, not yet 2 years old, which has brought

him to a spiritual crisis. He has a vision in which his daughter
is restored to life as a beautiful maiden adorned with pearls,
but she is separated from him by a stream. They enter into a
passionate and profound spiritual debate in which the Christian
faith eventually emerges triumphant. He tries to cross the stream
to join her, but, on touching the cold water, he awakes to find
himself stretched out on her grave.

'Cleanness' uses the stories of the Flood, Sodom and
Gomorrah and Belshazzar's Feast to explore the concept of
spiritual cleanness, while 'Patience' takes the story of Jonah and
the Whale to illustrate the virtue of patience. There is one stanza
in 'Patience' that gave me a warm sense of familiarity when I
first read it: when the whale vomits Jonah up on the shore and
the tide washes him up: 'he swepe to the sonde in sluchched [i.e.
dirty] clothes'. Where I spent my childhood there was a muddy
track known as 'slutchy lane' within yards of our house.

'Sir Gawain and the Green Knight' is the most celebrated of
the poems; the greatest Arthurian poem ever written. Unlike the
others, it uses pagan ideas to explain a Christian message. Two
ancient story elements are woven together: the Beheading Test
(Gawain chops off the green knight's head only to see him pick
it up by the hair and continue speaking!) and the Temptation
(the knight's wife's attempts to seduce him). The combination
makes for an enthralling tale.

Most readers, sooner or later, will want to tackle it in the
original, if only to feel the rhetorical power that alliterative verse
possesses. This passage, for example, describes the weather that
Gawain wakes up to on the day when he is to keep his bargain
with the green knight.

> ... Bot wylde wederes of the worlde wakned theroute
> Clowdes kesten kenly the colde to the erthe,
> Wyth nyye innoghe of the northe, the naked to tene.

The snawe snitered ful snart, that snayped the wylde;
The werbeland wynde wapped fro the hyghe
And drof uche dale ful of dryftes ful grete.

After Chaucer, the Gawain Poet is the greatest Middle English poet: the Chaucer of Cheshire.

THE NOSTRADAMUS OF CHESHIRE

The name of Robert Nixon, 'the Cheshire Prophet', has not been found in the parish records of his native Over, and some have doubted that he ever existed, but a firm belief in his prophecies used to be universal across the county and beyond.

> Passing through Cheshire lately, curiosity led me to enquire what credit these legends bore among the natives: and I was not a little surprised to find with what confidence they related

events which have come to pass within the memory of many of
the inhabitants; and how strictly they adhered to the notion that
he would not fail in the rest. (Anon)

Such was Nixon's enduring appeal that his birthplace, Bark
House, was preserved and maintained as a memorial for
centuries after his death. To call him 'the Nostradamus of
Cheshire' is, perhaps, an injustice to him, since his prophecies
pre-date those of the French seer and also those of Mother
Shipton.

At Whitsuntide in 1467, the wife of John Nixon gave birth to a
baby boy who was destined for great and enduring fame. Young
Robert was a startlingly ugly baby, and he grew into a fat boy
with a huge, misshapen head and goggle eyes. His personality
was no better, alas; sullen and taciturn, he could be taught
nothing, not even to look after cattle. If given a stick he would
lash out at oxen, chickens – even children – with the ferocity of
ignorance. One day, however, after a particularly long, brooding
rumination, he stood up and declared, in a harsh, grating voice:
'I will now prophesy!' Thereupon, dribbling as he spoke, he
spouted a long stream of doggerel verse before sitting down and
returning to his usual doltishness. The prophesies sounded like
gibberish, but others wrote them down and preserved them.

After the death of his parents, Robert was looked after by his
elder brother; an unenviable task, but he did succeed in teaching
Robert to handle the plough. The boy's cruelty to the animals
did not change, however. One day he was reprimanded for
scourging his brother's ox, and he replied, in an insolent tone,
that before long the animal would not belong to his brother
in any case. Three days later, the prophecy was fulfilled when
the Lord of the Manor claimed the ox as 'heriot' – a medieval
death-duty.

A string of similar local prophecies followed, all of them fulfilled in unexpected, riddle-like ways, but on 22 August 1485, Robert turned his attention to a national event.

On that date, he was ploughing a field with two oxen, but on this occasion, instead of poking them with his stick, he was seen to stop and address them, calling one 'Richard' and the other 'Harry'. He seemed to be watching some great event, while shouting: 'Now Richard! Now Harry! Now Harry, get over that ditch and you gain the day!'

As he spoke those words, far away, in a field near Market Bosworth in Leicestershire, Richard of York was making a valiant, if foolhardy, mounted charge towards Henry Tudor, only to be cut down and lose his crown. The victorious Henry was proclaimed king on the battlefield and messengers were sent out to spread the news. The village of Over was the one district where the result was not news; there, the locals already knew that they had a new king, and moreover, Nixon himself was able to describe the battle in detail.

A few weeks later, the prophet roused from his customary stupor and became horribly agitated. He had, he claimed, been summoned to appear before the king. Terror-struck, he ran up and down, protesting that he was to be sent to court where he would surely 'clem to death' (die of hunger). The neighbours sat down and laughed heartily at his antics. Even if his other predictions had come true, this, surely, had to be a joke – the idea that anybody, let alone the king, would want to meet their dirty, drooling village idiot!

A few days later, while turning the spit at his brother's house, Nixon shouted, 'He's coming! He's on the road, coming to get me!' Within an hour, there was a knock at the door; a messenger had arrived, demanding to see Robert Nixon, in the name of the king. The prophet's fame, it seemed, had travelled far.

Despite his protestations, Robert was taken to court and presented to the king, who ordered that his every utterance should be recorded for posterity. To calm his fears of starvation he was allowed to reside in the kitchen. Unfortunately, the charmless lodger soon made enemies of the cook and his staff by getting in the way, helping himself to bits of food and doing nothing useful in return. An officer, appointed by the king for Robert's protection, had no choice but to shut him away in a closet for his own safety. Soon after, this officer was summoned by the king and, in his eagerness to respond to the royal command, forgot to unlock the cupboard. There, Robert clemmed to death as he had foreseen.

Whether he existed or not, Nixon's reputation received a boost during the Jacobite rebellions, when both sides, Hanoverian and Jacobite, published pamphlets, carefully extracting those phrases that seemed to support their cause. The following verse, for example, was assumed to refer to the deposition and exile of King James II:

> When a raven shall build in a stone lion's mouth,
> On a church top beside the grey forest,
> Then shall a King of England be drove from his crown,
> And return no more.

However, the verse was back in the headlines in 1997 when ravens nested on Chester Cathedral, casting doubts on the future of Charles, Earl of Chester. Therein lies the problem, of course: the prophecies, like those of Nostradamus, are so ambiguous that they can be twisted to fit various purposes.

With that in mind, the reader might like to ruminate on the following six prophecies, all of which have been linked to events in British and European history, and see what comes to mind. The conventional interpretations are listed below.

Prophecies:

1. A time shall come when priests and monks
   Shall have no churches nor houses,
   And places where images stood,
   Lined letters shall be good,
   English books through churches are spread,
   Where shall be no holy bread.
2. I see men, women and children spotted like beasts and their
   nearest and dearest friends affrighted of them.
3. The great yellow fruit shall come over to this country and
   flourish and I see this tree take deep root, and spread into a
   thousand branches, which shall afterward be at strife with
   one another.
4. The weary eagle shall to an island in the sun retire,
   Where leaves and herbs grow fresh and green.
   There shall he meet a lady fair.
5. The dragons out of Ireland shall come and make war with
   England for their abomination so that London shall run with
   blood.
6. All sorts will have chimneys in their mouths.

Interpretations:

1. The Reformation.
2. The Great Plague of London 1665–66.
3. The coming of William of Orange, the inter-marriage of
   royal families and the First World War.
4. Napoleon's exile on the island of St Helena in 1815; a sunny
   island with lush vegetation, named after Helen of Troy.
5. The IRA bombing campaigns in London.
6. Not so many since the smoking ban!

THREE WITCHES

The belief in witches, or 'cunning women' and 'cunning men', in signs, tokens, and ghostly appearances, is so universal that it fails at first to strike you, from the simple fact that it is a recognized faith – a thing not to be remarked or made a wonder of … By no means to the lower class only is this confined. We heard such instances related by persons in a class, as it is phrased, of 'undoubted respectability.'

(The *Stockport Advertiser*, *c*.1850)

At that time there were people living within a few miles of Stockport who were considered, within their communities, to be witches and wizards, such as Old Becca of Whaley Bridge (then in Cheshire) and Bella Mottram, the last witch in Cheadle. There are tales of Bridget Bostock of Coppenhall, who could cure any ailment with spittle and a blessing, and Dick Spot, who could find anything that was lost or stolen. Alice Cawley lived in a low, thatched cottage in the Kelsall Hills with a toad that she kept on her bed (not *by* her bed, please note – *on* her bed!) as an aid to 'witching folk'.

None of these people sound like a real threat to the lives or souls of their neighbours and there are no reports of indictments against them. They had the good fortune to live in the nineteenth century, when belief in witchcraft, even if it was not confined to the lower class, at least was not shared by the legal profession. In the seventeenth century, however, it was shared by *everybody*, so announcements such as the following, though rare, were not considered unreasonable:

> Presentments by the jury that Margery Kendall, wife of David Kendall of Chester, labourer, on 20 February 1601/2 at Chester practised witchcraft on Joan wife of Gilbert Eaton from the 20 Feb to 1 March, so that the said Joan was in danger of her life.

Before going further, we need to dismiss the Hammer Horror notions of witchcraft trials from our minds, because modern research has blown many of those myths out of the water:

1. In England about 500 convicted witches were put to death over a period of 120 years, i.e. four or five per year – hardly the holocaust of the popular imagination.
2. Most of the witches that were brought to trial were acquitted; there is little evidence for 'witch hysteria'.
3. Those found guilty were hanged, not burned alive.
4. Records show that a significant minority of executed witches were male. At the Pendle trial in 1612, two of the eleven people condemned were men. Women, less involved with the official magic of church ritual, may, perhaps, have been more likely to resort to alternative forms, but a witch was not female by definition.
5. (Cestrians take note) Witches were not stuffed into barrels and rolled into the river Dee at Barrelwell Hill!

In Cheshire, the records of convicted witches can be counted on the fingers of one hand, and all date from the mid-seventeenth century. Two of them are from the same village, Rainow, near Macclesfield:

> That Ellen, wife of John Beech, late of Ranowe, in Cheshire, collier, on the 12th September, 1651, and on divers other days as well before as after, at Ranowe, did exercise and practise the invocacon and conjuracon of evil and wicked spirits, and consulted and convenated with, entertayned, imployed, ffedd and rewarded, certayn evill and wicked spirits.
>
> On the said 12th day of September the said Ellen Beech did exercise certain witchcrafts upon Elizabeth Cowper, late of Ranowe, spinster, whereby she, from the 12th till the 20th of September, aforesaid, did languish, and upon the said 20th day died.

On the very same day, Ellen's neighbour Anne committed the first of a string of offences:

> Anne, the wife of James Osboston, late of Ranowe, in Cheshire, husbandman, on the 12th day of September, 1651, practised certain wicked and divellish acts upon John Steenson, late of Ranowe, husbandman, which caused his death on the 20th of September.
>
> On the 30th of November, 1651, the said Anne Osboston used enchantments upon Anthony Booth, late of Macclesfield, in the county of Chester, gent., thereby causing his death on the 1st of April then next following.
>
> The said Anne Osboston on the 20th November 1653, at Ranowe, exercised certayn artes and incantacons on Barbara Pott, late wife of John Pott, of Ranowe, from the effects whereof she died on the 20th of January then next following.

And again on the 17th day of July, 1655, the said Anne Osboston practised sorceries on one John Pott, late of Ranowe, yeoman, from which time he languished until the 5th of August, when he died.

Note that both of these women were married, one of them to a 'husbandman', or free tenant farmer, perhaps even a landowner. This brings us to another myth: that a witch was simply a misunderstood, eccentric old dear, living quietly with a cat, condemned merely because she had a wart. In fact, they could belong to any class of society, rural or urban, young or old, married, widowed or single, male or female.

It is likely that the complaints were handed to the elders of Rainow parish church who, of course, were acquainted with both the accusers and the accused and knew very well who the magical practitioners in their community were. After several weeks of deliberation, they decided that there was a case to be heard. The Rainow Two were, therefore, taken to Chester for trial where they were joined by a third alleged witch, Anne Thornton, who had travelled a much shorter distance, from Eaton.

That Anne Thornton, late of Eyton in Cheshire, widow, on the 9th day of February, 1655, and on divers other days and times, as well before as since, at Eccleston, not having God before her eyes, but by the instigacon of the Divell beinge moved and seduced [did] with force and arms wickedly, divellishly, and feloniously exercise and practise certain divellish and wicked acts and incantacons called witchcrafts, inchauntments, charmes and sorceries in and upon one Daniell Ffinchett, sonne of Raphe Ffinchett, of Eccleston, yoman, beinge an infant of the age of three dayes, whereby he, the said Daniel from the 9th day of February in the year aforesaid until the 11th day of the same month, did languish, upon which said 11th day he the aforesaid Daniel by the said wicked and devillish acts soe by her the aforesaid Anne Thornton used, exercised and practised, as aforesaid, upon him the said Daniel, dyed.

Witch trials were heard by an experienced judge and a jury, but without prosecuting or defending lawyers. Accused and accuser(s) faced one another across the courtroom and exchanged testimonies in Jeremy Kyle fashion, after which the jury gave its verdict and the judge passed sentence. In this case, there were two judges: John Bradshaw of Congleton (*not* the John Bradshaw who sentenced King Charles I to death) and Thomas Fell. All three defendants pleaded not guilty but the jury found them all guilty and they were 'hanged severally by their necks' at Boughton on Wednesday, 15 October at about 3 p.m. The bodies were buried within three days, behind the church of St Mary on the Hill, in a place called 'Criminals' Corner', or so local tradition has it.

There is another Chester case. In 1663, a widow named Elizabeth Powell was arrested upon suspicion of witchcraft and was committed to the Northgate gaol where she died, six years later, after a long illness. It has been suggested that her accuser, Thomas Annion, blacksmith, hoped to get his hands on her land and possessions after her death, but that is not how the law operated; her worldly goods would have been confiscated by the state. Another point to note is that all of these alleged witches were accused, not by some deranged 'witchfinder general', but by their own neighbours. Superstition was universal, not imposed or encouraged by the authorities. In that century, even respected physicians thought that some ailments were caused by enchantment.

For that reason, I will not put the word witch in inverted commas as almost all modern writers do. They were not 'so-called' witches, nor were they followers of 'the old (pagan) religion'. They were, in fact, witches; they accepted the title and were recognised as such in their own communities. Beech, Osboston and Thornton were executed for murder, not for being witches. However impotent their spells, however coincidental the deaths of their victims, their malicious intent made them guilty according to the beliefs of the time. Demons were real beings, and to conjure them up, as Ellen Beech was alleged to have done, endangered the souls of her whole community.

Thankfully, the next century brought the Enlightenment, which swept all this nonsense away, didn't it?

Not necessarily. The following is taken from a broadsheet published between 1780 and 1820:

> Full and particular account of awful visitation of the Devil and six of his monsters which appeared to a party of young women foolishly and wickedly calling upon them to appear in the form of their intended bridegrooms, at Tranmere, on All Hallow Eve …
>
> … The master and mistress retired to rest about eleven o'clock, leaving the servants and their company to enjoy themselves as long as they thought proper. After perhaps drinking freely of the juice of grapes, besides other little nick-nacks in that way, they consented to try a scheme, the intention of which was to endeavour to see the faces of their intended lovers. They accordingly commenced by laying a table out with all the necessaries of life, with five chairs round it (there being five in the company): then they read the Lord's Prayer backwards, at the conclusion of which they hoped in the name of his Satanic Majesty, that their intended bridegrooms, would come and seat themselves at the table! No sooner had they uttered this, than their wish was complied with: it being about the hour of twelve, the doors flew open, and in an instant five ghastly looking gentlemen were seated round the table!!

The young women's fright was now heightened to a considerable degree at the sight of so awful a set of beings. They sat for little more than half an hour, when they arose, made their 'obedience', and disappeared as they came. Sarah Moseley was so much frightened that she died this morning, and little hopes are entertained of the recovery of the remainder.

Gallantry Bank, a hill near Bickerton, sounds like an echo of the age of chivalry, but is a smoothing over of Gallows-tree Bank. A murderer named Holford was hanged there in 1640.

THE HIGHWAYMAN FROM KNUTSFORD

The dashing highwayman Dick Turpin was an Essex man, and he ended his life in York, *but* did those feet in ancient times walk upon Cheshire's mountains green? Of course they did! He is supposed to have robbed a coach in a dark, hollow lane near Dunham Massey, then spurred Black Bess into a wild gallop across the fields to an inn at Hoo Green, where he took a swipe at one of the grooms with his riding crop and asked him the time, so as to set up an alibi. One romantic nineteenth-century writer reminisced:

When a boy I have often lingered by the side of the deep old road where this robbery was committed, to cast wistful glances into its mysterious windings; and when night deepened the shadows of the trees, have urged my horse on his journey from a vague apprehension of a visit from the ghostly highwayman. And then there was the Bollin with its shelvy banks, which Turpin cleared at a bound; the broad meadow over which he winged his flight; the pleasant bowling green of the pleasant old inn at Hough, where he produced his watch to the Cheshire Squires …

On another occasion he stayed at The Hawk Inn, Haslington, where he was once almost captured, but managed to scramble into the saddle and leap over the gate to freedom. The Saracen's Head at Warburton was a favourite hiding place; if the law came knocking, he could escape down a secret tunnel. In fact, he seems to have been a regular there; the initials D.T. are carved on one of the bedroom doors – what more proof do you need?

The mundane truth, of course, is that Turpin never visited Cheshire, and a good thing too, for he was a squalid, murderous thief who deserves to be forgotten. What I would like to know is: did any of our home-grown highwaymen come closer to the fictional image of the dashing, chivalrous, probably-good-looking-behind-the-mask, gentleman of the road?

In 1698, a few years before Turpin was born, Celia Fiennes rode, with two servants, from Tarporley to Whitchurch, via Beeston, Bulkeley, Hampton Heath and No Man's Heath:

There I think I may say was the only time I had reason to suspect I was engaged with some highway men. Two fellows all on a sudden from the wood fell into the road, they looked trussed up with great coates and as it were bundles about them which I believe was pistols, but they dogged me one before the other behind and would often look back to each other, and frequently jostled my horse out of the way to get between one of my servants' horses and mine ...

As it happened, the lady's luck was in – men were haymaking in the fields and it was market day in Whitchurch; with so many potential witnesses around, the highwaymen chickened out. I give them zero out of ten for chivalry and even less for dash.

Highwaymen could be a lot more dangerous than that, of course. In 1796, on a chilly January evening, a post-boy named Peter Yoxall was riding from Warrington to Chester, delivering the mail. The moon was full, so he found his way through Frodsham and Helsby easily enough, and by about eight o'clock was on a lonely road to the west of Dunham on the Hill. Coming round a bend, he saw two horsemen waiting at the side of the road. Frightened, he tried to gallop past them, but one of them grabbed his horse by the reins and snarled, 'Stop, or I'll blow your brains out!' The boy was only 15 years old, so the two men unhorsed him easily and tied him to a tree while they rummaged through the mailbag. Taking what they wanted, they galloped off, stopping for a drink at an inn in Tarporley, and another at the Griffin in Nantwich, before heading off southward.

Yoxall struggled with the rope and, after an hour and a half, freed himself, whereupon he ran to the nearest turnpike and called out the constable of Mickle Trafford.

Three days later, the highwaymen were both apprehended in a pub in Birmingham. At the trial, the 'learned judge, in a most pathetic manner, passed the awful sentence of death upon them.' While awaiting execution, both confessed to a long list of petty offences, and Brown wrote a short, penitential poem. Both bodies hung in chains at Trafford Green near the spot of the robbery – in the case of Price, for another twenty-four years! One spring, his skull provided a nesting site for a robin, which amused Egerton Leigh enough to pen these lines:

> Oh! James Price deserves his fate:
> Naught but robbing in his pate
> Whilst alive and now he's dead
> Has still Robin in his head.
> High he swings for robbing the mail,
> But his brain of Robin female
> Still is quite full; though out of breath,
> The passion e'en survives his death.

Price and Brown were certainly bolder than the boy that Celia Fiennes encountered, but still we have seen no courtesy, style or elan. Where might we find these qualities? Knutsford, perhaps?

In 1756, a new face appeared on the Knutsford social scene. Edward Higgins took up residence in the house that is now numbers 19–20 Gaskell Avenue and was immediately accepted by the local gentry as one of their own. Nobody knew where he had sprung from, but that hardly mattered: his elegant dress, refined speech and manners showed him to be a gentleman. 'Good breeding,' as Samuel Johnson observed, 'consists in having no particular mark of any profession, but a general elegance of manners.' Higgins certainly had no particular profession, but he had money enough to keep a stable of horses and make improvements to the house. His income evidently came from rents collected from the various properties that he owned in other parts of the country, for every so often, he would disappear for a month or two and return flushed with cash.

He married a respectable spinster named Katherine Birtles, and at the baptisms of his three sons and two daughters his occupation was each time recorded as 'gentleman'. 'Squire Higgins', as he soon became known, made many friends in the town, including Samuel Egerton of Tatton. He went hunting with them, drank and gambled with them, attended all the social gatherings and, in doing so, got to know the interiors of his neighbours' houses intimately. So, it was something of a shock for Knutsford society when, in 1767, they heard that their good friend had been hanged as a common criminal!

Higgins was, in fact, a thief, burglar, shoplifter and highwayman. Four years before coming to Knutsford, he had been tried at Worcester for sheep-stealing (then a hanging offence) but had been acquitted. Two years later he was not so lucky: found guilty of house-breaking, he was transported to the American colonies for seven years. His burgling skills were not forgotten, however; within a month of his arrival he broke into a house in Boston and came away with a very handsome profit. Having thus lined his pockets, he managed to board a ship for England and settled down in Knutsford, only three months after his transportation.

The tales about Higgins that were told in Knutsford portray him, perhaps, as a more lovable rogue than he actually was, but the basic facts are quite believable.

A man named Edward Hinchliffe related a story that was passed down in his family. His grandfather had once played a game of whist with Higgins, a Mr Egerton and another man. All four were snuff-takers, and they laid their snuffboxes on the table while they played. This was done partly for convenience and partly for display, because snuffboxes at that time were exquisitely ostentatious objects, intended to reflect the owner's wealth. In this case, Mr Egerton's box clearly outshone the other three. When it vanished, the public-spirited Higgins expressed great concern at the loss, and led the search tirelessly, earning the admiration of his companions for his diligence. The search was fruitless, of course; he had already hidden the box out of doors where he could collect it at his leisure.

In another story, we find Higgins attending a fashionable ball in Chester that broke up at three in the morning. Instead of going straight home, he took a stroll through the city's ancient rows and presently found himself among some of the finer houses on Stanley Street. One of the sash windows was open a little way and lit by a rush light. Thanks to some scaffolding and a ladder left by some builders, he managed to climb up to the window and peer through a gap in the curtains. A young girl walked in wearing a ballgown. She removed her jewellery and left it on her dressing table, then dismissed the maid and prepared for bed. Higgins waited until he was sure she was asleep, then edged the window open and crept in. As he was filling his pockets with jewels, she stirred, and he held his breath. The drowsy girl, thinking that her maid had come back in, groaned, 'Oh Mary! You know how tired I am, can't you put the things straight in the morning.' At that moment, her life hung in the balance, because Higgins later confessed that, had she sat up and seen him, he would have had to kill her.

On another occasion, our hero attended the county assembly in Knutsford, at which he was introduced to one Lady Warburton, who was dressed to impress and festooned with diamonds. He left the assembly early, mounted his horse and positioned himself at a quiet spot on the main road where he bided his time. He had a long wait, however, and when the lady's coach finally appeared, he was so unprepared that he had not even covered his face. The curtain was parted and Lady Warburton said, 'Mr Higgins! Why did you leave the ball so early?' The diamonds were safe.

When his friends thought he was rent-collecting, Higgins was robbing the public all over the west of England and South Wales.

It was only a matter of time before murder would be added to the list of his crimes, and it happened during a burglary in Bristol. The Stanley Street situation arose again, but this time he was discovered by a woman and her maidservant, and he killed them both.

The end of the road came in Carmarthenshire, in 1767, where he was caught breaking into a house and arrested. This time the punishment was not transportation, but death. Despite the ponderous list of his crimes, crowds gathered to protest against the conviction. Had they, perhaps, been reading the romantic Dick Turpin literature that had been circulating since his death twenty-eight years earlier?

There was to be a last desperate throw of the dice: a written reprieve came in the post. It was a very convincing letter, but the postmark proved it to be a clever forgery by an accomplice. When he heard that his ploy had failed, all the gentlemanly manners were cast aside:

> Higgins received this message with inconceivable insolence, treated the Sheriff with the most abusive language, for presuming to suspect and inquire into 'what was so evidently a truth.'

He declared that he would be torn in pieces rather than be led to the scaffold, but when the time came, he went meekly, 'in a very sullen humour'.

Higgins jotted down a confession of his crimes, which he handed over at the execution. In it, he expressed deep regret for the shame and disgrace he had brought to his family name and to his wife and children, who, he insisted were always unaware of his criminal activities. He provided them with a lump sum by arranging for his body to be sold to a London surgeon for dissection, so, immediately after the hanging, it was cut down and spirited away, but rather too hastily. As the autopsy began, the surgeon realised that Higgins was still – just – in the land of the living, so it was left to one of his students to carry out the execution.

Around 1809, Thomas De Quincy visited a museum in Manchester where he was shown a skeleton, believed to be that of the famous Knutsford highwayman. Over the forty or so years since his death, Higgins had received the Turpin treatment; his reputation had been airbrushed and the stories altered and embellished. De Quincy commented (with tongue firmly in cheek) that the man had 'ranked amongst the most chivalrous of his order, and was regarded by some people as vindicating the national honour in a point where not very long before it had suffered a transient eclipse'. He was referring to the fact that the highwayman idol of the previous century, Claude Duval, had been a French immigrant. This man's legend had been maturing for two and a half centuries and he was now revered as a saint. Duval had been courageous, handsome, well-dressed, a little addicted to gambling and womanising, perhaps, but such was his Gallic charm that women came to his trial and sobbed their hearts out.

Edward Higgins – the real Edward Higgins – was clever, resourceful, a flamboyant fraud, a conman of genius, a gentleman on the outside, a ruthless criminal on the inside. It does seem, however, that his settled family life in Knutsford taught him to care for his nearest and dearest, and made him a more complex and interesting character than Price, Brown or the real Turpin. He gets my vote.

Elizabeth Gaskell, who spent her childhood in a house only yards from that of Higgins, wrote *The Squire's Story* (1855), based on the tales she had heard about the famous highwayman.

THE ABORIGINE FROM MACCLESFIELD

6 July 1835. Port Philip Bay, Victoria, Australia.

A boatload of Englishmen comes ashore and sets up a camp near the beach. Some men of the local tribe spot them and come forward to present themselves, feigning friendliness, but plotting to send for reinforcements so that they can kill the newcomers and seize their belongings. Among these aborigines there is one who towers above the rest: 6ft 5in tall (or taller, according to some reports). He is paler skinned than the others, with black, shaggy hair, a low forehead, bushy eyebrows that obscure his small, deep-set eyes, a snub nose and skin scarred by smallpox. Were he not dressed, like the others, in a kangaroo skin and gabbling in the same impenetrable language, they might have taken him for a white man. He seems to be bursting to communicate with them but has not a word of English to help him. In desperation, he points to a tattoo on his arm: the initials WB. Then, one of the men offers him a little bread, saying the word 'bread' as he does so. The giant repeats the word back to him, not like a parrot, but like a man who is remembering something that he had almost forgotten.

They take him back to their camp and feed him boiled meat and biscuit, washed down with tea. One by one, other words come back to him and, within a few days, his mother tongue is back in his mouth and he is able to tell an astonishing story.

His name is William Buckley. He is a Cheshire man, born in Marton, near Congleton, in 1780, but brought up by his maternal grandfather in Macclesfield. At the age of 19, he left his apprenticeship as a bricklayer to join the army and saw action in the Netherlands, fighting against the French. The turning point in his life, however, came not in battle but in the barracks, where he was accused of handling stolen goods: a roll of cloth. Buckley claimed that a woman gave it to him and asked him to deliver it to a seamstress, to be made into clothing. His story was not believed, and the punishment was fourteen years at a penal colony in Australia. The ship delivered him, along with 300 other convicts, to Port Philip Bay in October 1803.

These men were among the first Europeans to set foot on this part of the continent. Life at the colony was almost unbearable, and escape attempts were commonplace. After two months of misery and hardship, Buckley and three other men decided to make their own bid for freedom. On a suitably dark night they seized a gun, a kettle, medical supplies and some food and ran off into the bush. One was shot and seriously injured, but the others kept running.

The plan was to head north-east, towards the settlement at Sydney, which they imagined to be a walkable distance away. Today, even with modern roads, it takes more than nine hours by car! Progress through the alien terrain was slow, they had little idea how to find food and Buckley's companions soon fell into despair; they decided that captivity and punishment were preferable to starvation and headed back whence they had come.

Buckley, though exhausted and dehydrated, chose to trudge onward around the bay for mile after mile, foraging for shellfish and berries and hiding from the native people, dingos, and the dangerous animals of his own imagination. It was several months before he reached the other side of the bay, and by then his body was covered in sores and walking was slow and painful.

His luck, however, was about to change.

One day, he noticed a spear sticking out of the ground, so he pulled it out and began to use it as a walking stick. Before long, he met some people who recognised the spear: it had belonged to Murrangurk, a well-respected leader of their tribe. He had died quite recently and, in accordance with local tradition, his spear had been used to mark the grave. They led the enfeebled stranger back to their huts and gave him a meal of fat, juicy grubs, which he found surprisingly palatable. Buckley had, at last, been rescued. He was with the Wathaurung people, whose territory stretched for 3,000 square miles – three times the size of Cheshire. There was a reason for their hospitality: they believed that white men were reincarnations of their own dead. This lanky stranger, holding Murrangurk's spear, must, therefore, be Murrangurk. 'To this providential superstition, I was indebted for all the kindnesses shown me,' he said, many years later.

The Wathaurung were a warlike tribe of hunter-gatherers, but over time, the Macclesfield bricklayer learned to fit in, even to feel at home. A diet of kangaroo, emu, possum and dingo meat helped him to recover his strength, and he soon learned to hunt and skin these animals himself.

Months passed. The reborn Murrangurk took a wife, lived as the others did, spoke their language, accepted their beliefs and took part in their rituals.

Years passed. He came to be respected as an Ngurungaeta, a revered spirit who was consulted on all important matters. The one-time soldier had found his true vocation as a peacemaker, a skilful defuser of volatile situations. Although he could handle the spear and boomerang as well as any, his Ngurungaeta status exempted him from taking part in any fighting. He watched their casual murders, blood-feuds and pitched battles from a safe distance and was a witness to cruelty and brutality that distressed him more than anything he had seen as a soldier. When the warriors dined on the roasted bodies of their defeated foes he declined to join them. For all the kindness the tribe had shown him, these were things to which he could never be reconciled, and, although he had forgotten every word of his mother tongue, he often found solace in Christian prayer.

Having recounted his tale, Buckley asked the Englishmen what year it was; only then did he realise that he had lived with the Wathaurung for fully thirty-two years.

The seamen had come to establish a settlement, a circumstance that was to stretch his diplomatic skills to breaking point. More pressingly, a great host of warriors had assembled, intent on murdering the strangers, including, should he choose to side with them, Buckley himself. Miraculously, he succeeded in buying enough time avert a massacre and, eventually, established peace, even friendship, between the two communities. The white men showered presents on the natives and, in return, were invited to a *corroboree* (a sort of spiritual knees-up).

The escaped convict was now a hero! The beautiful falls at Woorongo were named Buckley's Falls in his honour, and he was granted an official pardon for the little matter of the stolen cloth. He became invaluable to the settlers as an interpreter, and in doing so, played a major part in the downfall of the people who had nurtured him. Joseph Gellibrand, the Attorney-General of Tasmania, accompanied him on a journey back to visit his tribe. He wrote in his diary:

> February 5th 1836: I directed Buckley to advance and we would follow at a distance of a quarter of a mile. Buckley made towards a native well and after he had rode about 8 miles, we heard a cooey and when we arrived at the spot I witnessed one of the most pleasing and affecting sights. There were three men five women and about twelve children. Buckley had dismounted and they were all clinging around him and tears of joy and delight running down their cheeks ... it was truly an affecting sight and proved the affection which these people entertained for Buckley ... amongst the number were a little old man and an old woman, one of his wives. Buckley told me this was his old friend and with whom he had lived and associated thirty years.

As relations between the settlers and the aborigines soured Buckley's position became untenable, so he retired to Tasmania and married an Irish girl called Julia, so short next to him that they could not hold hands as they walked side by side. His astonishing run of luck finally ran out in 1856, when he fell out of a gig and was killed.

William Buckley was the inspiration for Alan Garner's novel *Strandloper*, which links the culture of the Aborigines with the folklore that he might have been aware of during his Cheshire childhood. His name also lives on in popular folklore: when Australians tell you, 'You've got Buckley's, or none' they mean you have little chance, or none whatsoever!

THREE HERMITS

The tiny hamlet of Plemstall consists of a farm, a cottage, a vicarage and a fifteenth-century church, which, when glimpsed from the train, appears to be stranded in the middle of flat fields, far from human habitation. It stands on a low eminence that, when the surrounding land was all marsh, kept it above the level of floodwater. In fact, there is a curious legend that this church was founded by a fisherman who was shipwrecked out at sea. A tremendous tidal wave carried him far inland until he reached this 'island', which saved him from drowning. In gratitude, he had the church built and dedicated it to St Peter, the 'fisher of men'.

The name Plemstall ('Holy place of Plegmund') contains another, more likely story. In the late ninth century a Mercian cleric and scholar of that name came here, intending to live the rest of his life as a hermit. A little dry hill surrounded on all sides by miles of watery wastes, it must have seemed to him the perfect place for a quiet life of study and contemplation. It was not destined to be, however; his learning had made him famous and, when Alfred became King of Wessex, he summoned Plegmund to his court, where he was put to work on various literary endeavours, such as an English version of Pope Gregory's *Regula Pastoralis*.

The Anglo–Saxon Chronicle tells us that in AD 890, 'archbishop Plegmund was chosen by God and by us all as archbishop of Canterbury'. It was a time of continual Viking attacks on England, yet he grew in stature, both as a bishop and as a politician, to become one of the best-loved men in the land. After his death he was canonised, and his reputation continued to grow with the centuries.

He did not leave Plemstall without leaving a trace, however. A legal document of 1301 mentions 'St. Plegmund's Well', and if you walk up the lane towards the church, you will find it on the left, just before the stone bridge. The well usually contains water, and, according to archaeologists, still has its medieval masonry. This is where he baptised converts in the ninth century and, I am told, there may be people still living who received baptism here in the twentieth century.

One summer in the 1990s, something mysterious and beautiful happened here. On the morning of 2 August – St Plegmund's feast day – a hawthorn tree that overhangs the well had been decorated with coloured rags and ribbons. It happened again in subsequent years and gradually evolved into an annual well-dressing ceremony performed by schoolchildren. The old man's memory is still alive.

*

The church of St John the Baptist, Chester, if old tales are to be believed, was once home to a Saxon hermit even more illustrious than Plegmund, and if you have ever been on one of Chester's popular ghost tours you may already know his name. A number of people claim, when walking home at night past the ruined arches at the east end of the church or taking a shortcut down

the 'haunted passage', to have seen a tall, robed, monk-like figure, walking among the ruins, under the trees, or staring out across the river. A few have passed close enough to exchange a few words, but the conversation is not mutually intelligible. The monk says things like:

'Spricest thu Englisc? La, on Godes naman, utan don swa us neod is, beorgan us sylfum swa we geornost magan, the laes we aetgaedere ealle forweorthan! God ure helpe!'

('Do you speak English? Look, in God's name, let us do what is necessary for us, defend ourselves as best we may, lest we all perish together. God help us!')

One man, having had such an exchange with the ghost, memorised a few of the strange words, parrot-fashion, and after some research, discovered that the language is, in fact, English; but a form of English that was spoken in the eleventh century.

So, who is this medieval monk, and what is he trying to tell us?

St John's church, for a twenty-year period in the eleventh century, was Chester's cathedral, but its roots go back much further than that. In AD 689, King Aethelred of Mercia was visited in a dream by an angel who instructed him to build a new church. He asked where in his wide kingdom it was to be, and the angel whispered, 'You will see a white hart standing in the place.' Some of the more weathered blocks of stone may be even older than that, for it is likely that stones taken from the nearby Roman amphitheatre were recycled by the original builders. Below the church, a high wall plunges down into a deep hollow; this was once a quarry where those same stones were quarried. There, seated on an outcrop of rock, is a Gothic-looking sandstone dwelling called the Anchorite Cell. It was built in the fourteenth century as a home for an anchorite – a hermit, or religious recluse – and restored, five centuries later, as a private house. Its first occupant, however, was (or had been) a King of England.

Gerald of Wales, in *The Journey through Wales* (1188), recorded that, in Chester,

… they maintain that King Harold is buried there. He was the last of the Saxon kings in England and, as a punishment for his perjury, he was defeated by the Normans in pitched battle at Hastings. He was wounded in many places, losing his left eye through an arrow which penetrated it, but, although beaten, he escaped to these parts. It is believed that he led the life of an anchorite, passing his days in constant attendance in one of the local churches, and so came contentedly to the end of life's journey.

You will notice an unsympathetic tone to Gerald's voice, which betrays the fact that, although born and bred in Wales, his ancestry was three-quarters Norman. The story of Harold's survival was still alive in the 1340s, when the Chester monk Ranulph Higden made a brief mention of it in his *Polychronicon*.

Before we mock the credulity of the medieval mind we might remind ourselves that some fans of the King of Rock and Roll hold a similar belief on much flimsier evidence. Besides, the team that found the body of Richard III in 2012 has recently turned its attention to this question: 'We found Dick, now let's find Harry.' Where should they dig this time? Perhaps that's what the ghost is trying to tell us.

*

The figure of the 'woodwose' was one of the main characters in medieval nightmares. In 'Sir Gawain and the Green Knight', we are told that Gawain had to fight them on his quest, along with ogres, dragons, wolves, bulls, bears and wild boar. The etymology of the name is similar to that of 'orang utan' in Malay: 'wild man of the woods'. To see just how hairy and scary they were, take a look at the misericords in Chester Cathedral; there are several examples, carved under the seats. Monstrous, but would that sort of thing give anybody a sleepless night as recently as 1809?

On 5 November that year, some young men from the village of Harthill were gathering wood to make a bonfire for Guy Fawkes Night. The sandstone hills of that neighbourhood are pocked with caves of all shapes and sizes, with names that titillate the imagination: Musket Hole, the Queen's Parlour and Mad Allen's Hole, where a nineteenth-century eccentric made his home. Most romantic of all are the Bloody Bones Caves beneath the towering Rawhead, once used by bandits who plundered the area, stealing cheeses and robbing graves. Seven of them were hanged in 1834.

The lads were quietly collecting branches near one of the caves when they got a sudden, visceral fright: a figure jumped out at them, a wild, hairy man, 'the frightfullest figure' they had ever seen. They fled back to the village where, wild-eyed, they babbled about the 'wild man' to anyone who would listen. Their story was believed, and four brave gentlemen promptly took up lanterns and followed their directions to the cave. Inside, they found the wild man, warming himself in front of a fire. He was a very old man, but he was tall, strongly built, and could move around the cave with great agility. His appearance was horrific, however, because since he had taken up that life he had neither cut his hair nor shaved, nor had his fingernails been trimmed, and as for his toenails, they had grown 'like unto asses hoofs'. The visitors sat down around the fire and asked him to tell them his story, which he did, in a voice that was remarkably strong for a man of his age.

The wild man had the surprisingly mundane name of John Harris. He had been born in the village of Handley in 1710, into a wealthy family that owned estates in Handley, Tattenhall and Broxton. Unfortunately, he was less lucky in love; his parents would not allow him to marry his sweetheart, Ann Egerton, whereupon he took a solemn vow never to marry and to have as little contact or conversation with mankind as possible. When his parents died, he sold off the estates and took up residence in dark, damp caves in the wooded hills. For more than twenty years, Harris lived in a cave in the grounds of William Leche of Carden, before removing to a similar abode on the Bolesworth estate. Here he lived for another forty-six years, with the owner's blessing.

The biggest surprise, perhaps, for the assembled gentlemen was to be introduced to Harris's manservant; a 69-year-old man named John Barlow who had lived in the cave next door and served him for fifty years!

This story was related in a broadsheet published in 1809, but by the end of the century most people dismissed it as fantasy. However, excavations of the Carden cave in the 1990s found evidence not only for occupation from the Palaeolithic era to the Bronze Age, but also scraps of eighteenth-century pottery and broken clay pipes. The walls inside have been made smooth, while in front of the entrance, a cobbled platform with post holes suggests that a timber porch had been erected. There is no doubt that the cave was inhabited in the 1760s.

THE OLD WOMAN OF DELAMERE

Where 'twixt the whalebones the widow sat down,
Who forsook the Black forest to dwell in the brown …
(Rowland Egerton Warburton, 1837)

In the summer of 1815, only a month after the Battle of Waterloo, two strangers appeared in Delamere Forest. A woman aged about 50 and her daughter were travelling in a donkey cart containing their few possessions. Walking alongside were two goats, whose milk had helped to sustain them on their journey.

The cart made its way to the front door of Vale Royal Abbey, where the mother presented a letter to Lady Cholmondeley:

> Madame, Madame, Thumley,
> At Vale Royal, Cheshire.
>
> Most Honerth, Highborn lady, my lady Thumley,
> As I have heard, that I am at the present tim, at your property, namly at the Oakmare, – We are latly, comen out of Germany, ware I lost my Husbunt. As I came into England, I vind rents so high, that I do not know how to do for to live, without Charaty, as the same way as most of the people live abroad, so I am gone about, to seek some waste ground, for then I can live, and provide for myself, for I have a little to make a small beginning with, but Halas! I vind that all the Commons are verbid. Now I am at rest, and this place I am able to live, if I may be there, but do not mean to make myself a Parish, for I never intent to submyt to Parish keping, for I belong to a foring chapel, in London, but I may yet do for myself, if I am permyted. Therefore, I humbly beg, Noble Lady, you would not denie me this favour, to stop here a few weeks, till I write up to London, for I cannot pay for lorging. I humbly beg, that your honour may send some of your trusty servants to enquire, and to see ware we are. We shall not trouble any body, or any thing, nor hurt, nor destroy any thing, rather protect the remanes of the trees, most noble Lady, I humbly beg, deny my not a little rest, at this peacable place. – I am,
>
> Your most obligint and humble stanger,
> MARIA HOLLINGSWORTH.

Permission was granted, and Maria put together a rough shelter of turves and branches on a bank near the mere. She found the two jawbones of a whale, which had been erected nearby as a curiosity, and used them to support the roof, much as crucks

A PERTITION OF A KIDD

were once used in half-timbered houses. The forest was then an unfrequented wilderness, but the strangers eventually attracted notice. Their dress marked them out as 'frem folk' – foreigners, or at any rate, people from outside the county. At first, opinion was divided: some called her The Lady of Oakmere, others, The Oakmere Witch. According to one rumour, she was none other than old Boney himself, disguised in women's clothes, plotting another comeback after his recent defeat and downfall. In time, however, she gained acceptance and became known to her neighbours as 'Mary Ann'. A man who met her wrote:

> The poor woman's appearance bespoke great poverty, but her miserable garments were tidy, and did not conceal the faded remains of beauty; her manners and language were evidently very much above her present wretched situation …

She improved the turf dwelling by raising the walls and adding a door and a window. After the donkey died, its hide was stretched over the roof to make it more watertight. Even then, her home was no more than a single room, 10ft by 8ft, and about 5ft high. Flowers, fern fronds and pebbles were collected, magpie-like, and used for decoration.

She was able to enclose half an acre for a garden, the produce of which her daughter would sell on Tarporley market. Visitors of all social classes came to offer charity; one donated some warm clothes, another, a few chickens. Aware of the dangers of life in the forest, Maria also acquired a guard dog and a pair of pistols, declaring that she would not hesitate to shoot any nefarious rascal who might approach her home.

The 'few weeks' of Maria's intended stay turned to a few years. The little hut became the daughter's schoolroom: her mother taught her English, German and French. Their solitude was to be disturbed, however. The forest had been enclosed, which meant that local people were now at liberty to settle in the forest. A few humble cottages sprang up nearby: Maria had neighbours at last. At first, relations were good: seeing that these families could not afford education for their children, she gave them free lessons in reading and writing. Little by little, however, the mood was changing. People began to say that Maria was odd, awkward, difficult to deal with, even delusional, paranoid. Had social isolation affected her mind?

In 1820, a letter arrived from her son in Hanover to say that he was embarking for Liverpool and would come to visit her in the forest. Thrilled at the prospect of seeing him, mother and daughter selected a high vantage point where they took turns to keep watch. After many disappointments, they saw a man approaching through the trees and both were convinced that it was him. They called his name, but he seemed not to hear and, instead of coming to their hut, he knocked on the door of a nearby cottage, as if to ask directions. The occupier invited him inside and, although Maria watched the house until nightfall, he did not re-emerge. The householder, unfortunately, was one of Maria's sworn enemies, so she felt unable to approach the house. During the night, however, she crept out and, by the light of a full moon, saw her enemy and his son carrying a body in a sack which they dumped in the mere, making a loud splash. Finding the water too shallow, however, they each grabbed a spade and carried the body off into the forest, returning later with the empty sack. She was in no doubt that her son had been murdered and buried.

She told her story to a local magistrate, Mr George Wilbraham, who organised a thorough search of the area. Nothing was found there, but, soon after, a corpse was fished out of the water, not at Oakmere, but Marbury Mere, about 15 miles to the south. Maria was taken to identify the body and confirmed that it was her son. Meanwhile, Mr Wilbraham had written to a contact in Hanover who replied with the news that Maria's son was alive and well and had not yet embarked for Liverpool! It was several weeks before he found his way to the hut in the forest, and when he did, he was instantly recognised by mother and sister. A happy ending? Sadly, no, because although at first overjoyed to see her son, Maria now had to face the fact that the 'murder' in the forest had happened only in her imagination. Her mental conflict finally resolved itself with a reversal of opinion: she decided that she had been right about the murder and that this young man was an imposter! By this time, he had left to work as a carpenter in Manchester while her daughter had gone into service in London.

Maria continued with her sequestered life until old age and illness forced her to seek help; her London friends found her a place in the Dutch almshouses in the city.

Before leaving Oakmere in 1829, she remembered the kindness of Lady Delamere with two gifts: a German prayer book, and a goat – the last descendant of those she had brought with her fourteen years earlier. A dedicatory verse was attached:

THE PERTITION OF A KIDD

A lonesome stranger creves a boon,
To rove within the shade;
In jour spacious park allone,
And hopes jour frendly ade.
My frendly dame is going to leve
The place ware I did dwell:
I humbly begg do me resieve,
And use a Stranger well.
Then I will in return agien
Cheer jour lonesome walk;
In als my nature still remane,
And in innocence with you talk.

A M HOLLINGSWORTH, Oakemere

In 1832, in her late sixties, Maria wrote an account of her life that explained how circumstances had brought her to such a strange existence. She was born in 1765 at Leeuwarden in west Friesland, the daughter of a Lutheran clergyman. She married an English soldier and followed him through campaigns in Germany until he was killed at the Siege of Bergen op Zoom in 1814. As a war widow with a son and daughter, she qualified for a small pension from Charlotte, the German-born Queen of England, who had set up a charity for 'distressed Germans' who were living in England. While her son became a carpenter's apprentice in Hanover, she and her daughter left for England in search of a permanent home. That proved difficult to find, as one parish after another moved them on, so she resolved to try America, and therefore headed for the port of Liverpool. Delamere Forest lay on her road, and that brings us back to the beginning of our story.

There is one conundrum, however, that has never been solved. In 1832, one of Maria's Cheshire friends visited her at the almshouse in London and found her living, at last, in a good-sized room full of knick-knacks, one of which was a little model of her old hut. Her daughter happened to be present and gave the impression of intelligence and level-headedness, yet, when asked about her brother she insisted that her mother was right: the man was not her brother. Moreover, he had tried to seduce her and even asked her to marry him; what brother would do that? Was she sincere, or was she loyally protecting her mother?

What, I wonder, became of Maria's forest home? It may have been pulled down and destroyed; or was it, perhaps, simply left to fall apart and become buried under leaf-litter?

I suspect the latter fate, because when T.A. Coward discussed Oakmere in his 1932 book *Cheshire*, he wrote:

> A short time ago, during rebuilding of the keeper's cottage, a huge mammalian bone was unearthed; it proved to be part of the jaw of a large whale, probably the now extinct Greenland right whale, which had evidently been brought and used as a gatepost base by someone in the neighbourhood; we can guess a retired whaler, for at Whalebone Cottage on the road near is a whale-jaw archway.

Good guess, but wrong!

GYPSIES

It was in 1514 that they were first noticed in England: dark-skinned foreigners dispersing to all parts of the country: Egyptians, as they were called. Thirteen years later, they had reached Cheshire. In 1527, Thomas Cromwell wrote:

> To my Lorde of Chestre, president of the Counsaile of the Marches of Wales, regarding *Egipcyans*, who spoiled, robbed and deceived. Ye shall compell them to repair to the next porte of the see to the place where they shal be taken, and eyther wythout delaye upon the first wynde that may conveye them into any parte of beyond the sees to take shipping, and to passe to owtward partyes, or if they shall in any wise breke that commaundement without any tract to see them executed …

However, Cheshire, as Cromwell knew, was not like other counties. It was still a palatinate, with, to some extent, its own legal practices, and a long history of turning a blind eye to lawless incomers from England. The south-west of the county was a particular haven, as place names such as Noman's Heath and Robberhill might suggest. East of Farndon was a boggy region called King's Marsh, which belonged to no parish and had no owner save the Crown. Here, gypsies, foreigners, and outlaws were tolerated, so long as they did not build 'any fixed houses by the means of nails or pins, save only booths and tents to live in'.

Other sanctuaries were Hoole Heath, near Chester and Rudheath, near Goostrey. Threapwood, a little community on the Welsh border, is respectable enough today, but in days gone by it was a last resort for military deserters, dubious characters, squatters and ladies of blemished morals. The name means 'disputed wood', and within that wood there were no parish rates or land tax to pay, and justices of the peace could do nothing. From the gypsy's point of view, Cheshire was (to borrow a Romany word) *kushti*.

The centuries rolled by and the 'Egyptians' became ever more anglicised, but some customs died hard: even in the nineteenth century, many of Cheshire's Romanies preferred not to stray too far outside the county. In 1882, a correspondent to *The Cheshire Sheaf* wrote of a chance meeting at Haughton, near Bunbury. Under a hedge, he encountered:

… the usual donkey-cart, blanket-tent, and campfire, which mark the English Gipsy's home. After dinner we sauntered down by star-light to smoke a pipe at the camp fire, and were saluted by a very Queen of Gipsies. She had evidently once been a handsome woman; and was still tall, upright as a dart, and of powerful frame, with hair yet black, though short, and turned behind the ears. The eyes, though small and sunken, had still much of the fire of earlier days; and the hands, with gold rings on the first and third fingers, had still a grip which would hold any burglar a prisoner! She wore a print dress, with a red handkerchief round her neck, and had no covering for the head. Round her neck was a chain suspending two lockets, and some beads. A cheerful fire of wood was burning, and close beside was a small tent made of eight withy sticks, with ends stuck into the ground and bent over at a height of five feet, so as to support the blanket covering. A heap of straw sufficed as bed; a four-wheeled donkey-cart covered in, but without a fireplace, was the sleeping room of the woman and her grand-daughter, the son occupying the little tent. We sat down for a talk, and she told us something of her life. I took out pencil and paper, and wrote from her own lips as follows:

'My name is Lucy Taylor. I was a Boswell [a common gypsy name in Cheshire and parts of Wales] before I was married – I am now a widow ... I don't know how old I am. I was only once married, and was then 16 years old. We broke the stick over the fire, in gipsy fashion, to get married. I have had 16 children, and have about 50 grandchildren ... I have travelled about all my life, and my father and mother before me: my father was 105, and my mother 106, when they died. Two and a half years was the longest I ever was in a house in my life; I was never out of England, or London way, but always in these Northern parts. Me and that grandchild, and my son, live together: we make baskets and clothes pegs, and sell them. I was out all last winter round about Chester, and you know how cold it was, and yet I never had a fire in the van to sleep by. We go eight or ten miles a day. Father and Mother brought me up this way, and I like it better than a house: I could not do with a house – the way you are brought up is the way you like. I cannot read or write, and I don't think I was ever at school: not many Gipsy people have been in school, you see, they are here today, and gone tomorrow! We came from Waverton today and shall move on towards Northwich tomorrow, and get back to Chester towards Christmas.'

In another issue, a researcher was looking through some old wills and found one, dated 1627, that appeared to be the inventory of a gypsy who had settled in the parish of Crewe, near Farndon, very close to King's Marsh. The list of his possessions is as short as one would expect: a cart with furniture, a mare with its saddle and harness, tools, baskets, clothes, boots, a sword, a dagger, and a few other trifles. The man's name, Rumwell Durbare (or Rumballe Durbarre), was so unusual that the writer assumed it to be of gypsy origin and appealed for advice from other readers. In the next issue, a reader from Wrenbury sent in a reply:

Lilengri Palor Earwaker te Hughes, – Dikdum boot Romani divvusor. Kanna tarno keray, dikdum boot Boswellundy opray

drummer adray Yorkshire. Kanaw, pooroder adray Cheshire
Tem, shunaw booti Romani lavvor te navvor, – kekke Durbarre.
Mawr pooker mandi Rumbold Durbarre se Romano Nav, pooro
y nevvo; mawr pen ajaw: mawr tchiv lesti apopli adray lillor: me
jinaw ferrader. O Romano mush se kekke Kerjivver, Givengro,
Kalengro, dra poori beshor. O Nav Durbarre, – se lesti Peerdu,
Posh Romano? Kek pooro Romano rut: me jinov duvvaw.
Romano Foki kidivvus, adray, adray covvo Cheshire Tem,
lelenna Lee nav. Dra sor meeri merriben me kekke shundum
Durbarre, Romano nav: kekke, kekke. O Romano Krallas,
Aaron Lee, suvella aky, adray meero Congry-poov. Booti unli
Romano Foki, Mush te Monishny. Dada Dy te tchavvy, venna
kidivvus te janna odoy; peerenna adral leskro mullino ker;
dikenna sawr suvella, o pooro Krallas, apallo Congry-poov-
tchaw, divvus te rati, tatto te shillo, kindo te shukko, besh te
besh. Pardel, opray leskro mullino burr, o Gorjiko Congry-Ry
tchivdas kooshki lavvor avree Divvuleskro Lil. Dawdy! Dawdy!
Kushko Bok, Gorjiki Palor. – Kushko Bok, Lilengri.

Pen tatchopen adray lillor. Tchitche se ferrader.

T.W.N.

The language is, of course, Romany, and it was not long before
another reader provided the following translation:

Book brothers Earwaker and Hughes, [editors of the
publication] – I saw many Gipsies [in former] days. When
[I was] young at home, I saw many Boswells on the roads in
Yorkshire; Now [that I am] older in Cheshire Land, I hear
many Gipsy words and names, – not Durbarre. Do not tell me
Rumbold Durbarre is a Gipsy name, old or new; do not say so:
do not put it again in books, I know better. The Gipsy man is
no house-dweller, farmer, cheesemaker, in old years. The name
Durbarre, is it Tramp, Half-Gipsy? No old Gipsy blood: I know

that. Gipsy people today, in this Cheshire Land, take Lee [as a] name. In all my life I never heard Durbarre [as a] Gipsy name: no, no. The Gipsy King, Aaron Lee, sleeps here, in my church-yard. Many amongst the Gipsy people, man or woman, fathers, mother, and children, come to-day to go there; they walk through his vault [dead-house]; they see all he sleeps, the old King, under the churchyard grass, day and night, hot and cold, wet and dry, year and year. [More] over, on his dead stone, the non-gipsy minister [lit. Church-gentleman] put good words out of God's book. See! See! Good luck, non-gipsy brothers; good luck, authors!

Tell truth in books. Nothing is better.

Most gypsies of the time were illiterate, of course, so 'T.W.N.' was unusually well-educated.

How many gypsies live in Cheshire today? A 2006 study estimated that there are 1,300–1,400 gypsies living in caravans on sites across the county, in addition to the unknown number now settled in houses. Three-quarters of them identify themselves as Romanies.

And how much of the old 'black blood' flows in our own veins, I wonder? As T.W.N. says, most Cheshire gypsies adopted the surname Lee, and, in a county where Leigh is one of the commonest names ('as many Leighs as fleas', according to an old rhyme), one might wonder how many of those Lees now spell their name as Leigh.

Kushko bok, Romano foki!

THE SLEEPER UNDER THE HILL

The following tale has been passed down through the generations in north-east Cheshire.

A Mobberley farmer who had fallen on hard times decided, with a heavy heart, that he must sell his horse. It was the finest in the district, a handsome white mare, young, strong and intelligent, but he could no longer afford to keep it. Such a horse, he reasoned, would fetch a high price at Macclesfield market, so, one morning in late October he mounted it and set off on the 10-mile journey. Before long, he came to the village of Chorley, and, soon after that, the escarpment of Alderley Edge loomed into view, like a long, wooded barrier, blocking his path. He had to make a choice: should he go the long way around or choose the more difficult, but shorter route over the edge?

The sun was already high in the sky, so the farmer decided upon the latter course. He dismounted and led his horse up the steep, sandy slopes, through bracken and bilberry, until he reached a place called Thieves' Hole. Here, he tied the horse to a tree and lay down in the heather to take a short rest. From here, the Cheshire Plain was laid out before him like a coloured tablecloth; beyond, blue in the distance, he could make out the mountains of Wales.

A shadow passed across him. Looking up, he saw a tall man standing nearby, dressed in a long cloak with a gnarled staff in his hand.

'You are going to the market,' said the stranger, in a deep, clear voice.

'How did you know that?' asked the farmer.

'You mean to sell your horse there.'

The farmer got to his feet and looked the stranger up and down. Who was he? Where was he from? How was he able to read his mind? Was he, perhaps, a wizard?

'It is a fine horse. I will buy it from you.'

'Ah, but I wunna sell it!'

'But you are taking it for that purpose! Come, I'll pay you a better price than any you would get at market.'

The farmer stopped to think. By accepting the offer, he could make a bigger profit and save himself a journey. It was tempting, but could this outlandish-looking fellow be trusted? He made a firm decision.

'No, I'll offer it at market and nowhere else. If you want it, you mun come and bid wi' the rest.'

'As you wish, but I tell you, nobody will buy your horse at the market today.'

The robed stranger turned and was out of sight as quickly as he had appeared. The farmer sat down for a few minutes, feeling confused and shaken, but at last recovered himself and set off again.

At Macclesfield he found the market in full swing – in fact, he had never seen it so busy or so noisy. Farm animals of every kind were for sale, from cattle, sheep and pigs down to hens, geese and ducks, but, surprisingly, not a single horse was on offer. All the better, he thought: no competition! He found a good, prominent position where he and his horse could be seen by all and waited for the buyers to make their bids. Strangely, however, nobody so much as glanced at his fine horse, even though the cattle were fetching high prices, sheep and pigs were selling like hotcakes, and geese and ducks were being carted away in dozens. He began to wonder if anyone could see him or hear his voice. The day passed, deals were done and, one by one, every last animal was sold and led away, down to the last scraggy hen. The crowds went home, stalls were dismantled and packed away, until all that remained in the market place was the sad figure of the farmer, standing with his beautiful but unwanted horse.

There was nothing for it but to return home, so he mounted his horse again and set off back to Mobberley. It was growing dark when he reached the Edge, and a ferocious wind was raging through the battered trees and flinging crows about the sky like rags.

When, again, he reached Thieves' Hole he saw a tall figure, silhouetted against the grey sky, and he knew, instantly, who it was. His first impulse was to dig in his spurs and ride on, but curiosity made him pause.

'Well,' said the wizard, 'no one wanted your horse, did they? You could have saved yourself a lot of time and trouble if you had let me buy it this morning. Will you sell now?'

'Maybe … or maybe not.'

'Mark my words, no one but me will ever buy your horse.'

'Why not?'

'Because it is needed. Dismount and follow me. I will show you.'

He led the farmer along a winding path through the trees until, at last, they were confronted by a gigantic rock. A single, sharp tap with his staff caused it to split open, revealing a set of iron gates. Another tap and the gates opened to reveal a tunnel, leading to an immense, echoing cavern. The wizard again tapped his staff against the rock and the entire cave was illuminated. The farmer was awestruck by what he saw. On one side, armoured knights lay slumbering in regular rows, and, in the midst of them, a king, wearing a golden crown. On the other side, white horses slept in their stalls.

'Who the heck are this lot?' asked the farmer in a trembling voice.

'That is the great King Arthur and those are his knights. They have slept under this hill for many centuries, but one day, when England is in her greatest need, they will awaken.'

Then the farmer noticed something irregular: one of the stalls was empty. One more horse was required.

The wizard whispered in his ear: 'Now will you sell?'

The farmer gazed at the spectacle before him. Could he condemn his horse to sleep for centuries in this cave? It was pulling on the bridle, champing at the bit, its eyes wild with alarm.

'Never!' he shouted, and the word echoed across the cave as he mounted his horse and galloped back through the tunnel and out into the fresh air. It took him many hours to find his way in the darkness and dawn had broken by the time he reached home.

The farmer never tried to sell his horse again, and, although he visited the Edge many times after that, he could never find the path he had taken, or the great rock.

And the king? He slumbered on under the hill, as he does to this day.

Folklorists call that story 'The Sleeping Hero', or 'The Sleeper Under the Hill'. Variants of the myth – a national hero and his warriors asleep under a particular hill, waiting to rescue their country in its hour of need – have been recorded from many other countries. In Ireland he may be Fionn mac Cumhaill, in Wales, Bran the Blessed, and in Europe, Charlemagne, William Tell, Vlad the Impaler, etc.

In some variations, a herdsman wanders into a cave in search of a lost animal and stumbles upon the sleepers. Sometimes the hero awakes and asks a cryptic question, such as:

'Do eagles still fly around the mountain top?'

'Yes.'

'Then it is not yet time,' and he resumes his slumber.

The ubiquity of the myth suggests that it belongs to an ancient oral tradition. My re-telling is based on literary sources; I didn't learn it at my grandfather's knee as a child. However, novelist Alan Garner, whose Alderley Edge roots run deep, did learn it that way, and his telling of the tale differs from the literary sources on a few points:

1. There are, for some reason, 149 knights and 148 horses.
2. The farmer agrees to sell his horse and is paid with treasure taken from the cave.

3. The tall stranger is not described as a wizard.
4. The king is not named as Arthur; that may be a romantic Victorian addition to the story.

To see what a great writer can do with such material, read Garner's novel *The Weirdstone of Brisingamen*, and if you want to understand the legend more deeply, you must read his essay 'Oral History and Applied Archaeology in East Cheshire'. I will not spoil your pleasure by saying any more here.

> If you take the path along the Edge from the Beacon to Stormy Point, you will come to a circle of stones, which has become known as the Druidic Circle. This mystic monument was put there by Alan Garner's great-great-grandfather, a stonemason who had a few stones he wanted to get rid of!

3

BEAUTY

THE CENTRE OF CHESHIRE

There are many claimants for the title 'biggest oak tree in England', and one of the most deserving is the old tree at Marton, north of Congleton. By biggest, I mean fattest, of course, not tallest; the trunk, now hollowed out, once measured 58ft in circumference. The cavity inside has been used, in the past, as a shippon for a bull and as a storehouse for farm implements. These days, it is split into three parts, but they share a root system, so they may still be regarded as one tree. The Marton oak is also one of the oldest in existence – older, perhaps, than Cheshire itself. If the tree-dating experts are right, it had already reached its first century when King Alfred's son Edward the Elder created the new county of Cestrescir in AD 920. This is the only oak I know whose acorns are sold as souvenirs – even if the price is only 10p!

Davenham

At Bostock Green, there is another oak that makes a different claim. It stands at the roadside, marking, they say, the exact centre of the traditional county of Cheshire. This one is not much more than 130 years old, but it inherited the title from an earlier oak that stood on the same spot for centuries. In 1887, when the old tree was a rotten, crumbling stump, it was felled, and, since it was the year of Queen Victoria's Jubilee, a new one was planted as part of the celebrations. This is now a handsome, spreading tree, with a plaque declaring its claim.

But ... in the village of Davenham, just a couple of miles to the north, they will have none of it! The steeple of their church, they maintain, marks the centre of Cheshire 'within three barleycorns'. William Smith, in 1656, wrote of 'a parish church of stone, with a spire-steeple, called Davenham, which standeth in the very middle of Cheshire, as near as I can guess; it may, peradventure, lack an inch, or more.'

The only way to resolve this question would be to print the map of the county onto card, cut it out with nail scissors and balance it on the point of a pencil to determine the exact spot, but who would waste his time on such an exercise?

My pencil point gives us a clear winner. The centre of Cheshire is – (drum roll) – the steeple of Davenham church! (cheers and triumphant applause.)

WHAT'S THE WEATHER LIKE?

In 1938, Arnold Boyd wrote in *The Country Diary of a Cheshire Man*:

There is a poet who wrote in praise of the South Country, and Hilaireously described the Midlands as 'sodden and unkind' and declared that the skies of North England were 'fast and grey'.

Cheshire may be claimed by the Midlands or the North, for it belongs to both, and should invite the poet to pay the county a visit while the meadows are still green and dry and the skies are blue. He might alter his opinions; not that we really mind what those who live in the South Country think of us!

Belloc's attitude is far from dead even today: here, for example, speaks another southerner, the late A.A. Gill:

> In the middle distance cows set their noses to the north and watch the battleship-grey clouds roll in. This part of the country gets more rain than anywhere else in Britain. It trundles in from the Atlantic, remorselessly pissing on Cheshire's fireworks.

In fact, those south-westerlies piss most of their rain on the Welsh mountains before they reach us, and much of what remains is saved for the Pennines. The relatively dry climate of central and eastern England reaches a north-western outpost in the Cheshire Plain. Our eastern hills, admittedly, share the cooler, damper climate of the Peak District of which they are a part, but even that region is a parched desert compared with Snowdonia. Yes, there is rain enough to keep the grass so lush that cows may graze until October, but sodden and unkind? No.

The western half of the county is drier, warmer and sunnier than the eastern half, the tip of Wirral being the balmiest (and the windiest) of all. Winters are too mild to bring much snow, but when it does fall we blame it, like so many other things, on the Welsh: 'They're pluckin' their geese in Wales and sendin' their fithers here.'

I shall give the last word to the Farndon-born John Speede (1551–1629):

If the affection to my natural producer blind not the judgement of this my survey, for aire and soile it equals the best and farre exceeds her neighbours the next Counties: for although the Climate be cold and toucheth the degree of latitude 54, yet the warmth from the Irish Seas melteth the Snow and dissolveth the Ice sooner there than in those parts that are farther off; and so wholesome for life that the inhabitants generally attaine to many yeares.

IS CHESHIRE FLAT?

We can resolve this one with an imaginary car journey, west to east, across the county.

Driving from West Kirby to Chester takes us through pleasantly undulating country with rocky outcrops of sandstone and views over the Dee estuary. Not very flat so far.

East of Chester the landscape levels out into flat fields bordered by low hedges and straight ditches. Agreed, this is flat, but look – there are hills only a few miles ahead of us. This is the Mid-Cheshire Ridge which runs north to south, cutting the Cheshire Plain in two. Its highest point is Raw Head which stands ... ooh, at least 745ft above sea level. You may laugh, but near the village of Willington is a place called by the locals 'Little Switzerland'. All is relative, as they say. The Boot Inn is conveniently situated in the foothills; here you can down a pint and perhaps procure ropes and ice axes before climbing further.

Beeston Castle provides a fine vantage point to survey both halves of the Plain. Away to the west it is framed by the overlapping outlines of the Clwydian Hills, and perhaps, 'battleship grey' clouds permitting, the mountains of Snowdonia beyond. Turning to the east we see the distant Derbyshire hills, right?

Wrong! This is a mistake that generations of people have made – perhaps because of our habit of using labels like 'the Cheshire Plain' and 'the Derbyshire Peak':

> I have an impression that many dwellers in central and west Cheshire are in the habit of calling this range the 'Derbyshire Hills.' I doubt extremely whether a single yard of Derbyshire can be seen out of Cheshire. From Lyme Cage to Shutlings Low, the whole range belongs to my native county. (J.C. Liverpool, 1896)

Our virtual journey takes us that way, into the Peak District National Park, but we will not be crossing the Derbyshire border. Continuing eastward, the land rises steadily, until, around Congleton, it starts to roll. To the south of us is Mow Cop and, to the east, Bosley Cloud raises its misty head. Both are over 1,000ft, but they are molehills compared to what is to come. The Buxton road leads us by many twists and turns into the real hill country where the trees and hedges give way to heather, cotton grass and dry-stone walls. The pointed peak of Shutlings

Beeston Castle

Low looms into view – nicknamed (to the merriment of Alpine visitors) 'The Matterhorn of Cheshire'. We are now 1,659ft above sea level. Turning northwards, we finally reach Shining Tor, which, at 1,833ft (559m), is the highest point in the modern county of Cheshire. Only nine of England's forty-eight counties can boast a higher point. A.E. Housman's 'blue remembered' Shropshire hills cannot top it, for we are higher than Brown Clee Hill, and far higher than anywhere in the Cotswolds. And what of the celebrated Downs, described by Belloc as 'The Great Hills of the South Country'? Their highest peak stands a mere 886ft (270m); in Cheshire, we can sit comfortably in the Cat and Fiddle pub and know that we are nearly twice as high! Cheshire's hills may not have been eulogised by poets, but they deserve to be.

Shining Tor was not always Cheshire's highest peak. Prior to 1974, when Longdendale formed the handle of the teapot, we could claim Black Hill, standing at 1,909ft. Today it is West Yorkshire's highest point.

THE HEADLESS CROSS

Urchins' Kitchen, in the Delamere Hills, is a remarkable rock formation where (if we take the name literally) hedgehogs cook their meals. It is a gorge in the sandstone, gouged out during the last Ice Age by meltwaters flowing beneath the ice. The stone is soft and, over many years, visitors have honoured it with their carved initials – or perhaps the hedgehogs just get bored while waiting for the microwave to go 'ping'!

We have double standards about this form of vandalism. At Leche House, Chester, someone used a diamond ring to inscribe the words 'Charming Miss Oldfield 1736' on one of the tiny windowpanes, while the windows of the nearby Yacht Inn (demolished in the 1960s) boasted a couplet composed, and scratched onto a window, by Jonathan Swift himself:

Rotten without and mouldering within,
This place and its clergy are all near akin.

Even the multi-mullioned windows of Little Moreton Hall were not sacred:

Man can noe more know weomen's mind by kaire
Then by her shadow hede ye what clothes shee weare.

These three acts of desecration are now regarded, respectively, as a romantic gesture, a piece of poetical wit, and a wry comment on human nature. The passage of time softens our attitude.

T.A. Coward made a pilgrimage to these hills while researching his book *Picturesque Cheshire* (1903). He was seeking information about the 'Headless Cross' that featured in one of the prophecies of Robert Nixon:

A crow shall sit on top of Headless Cross,
In the forest so grey,
And drink of the nobles' gentle blood so free.

It was marked on maps in 1819 and 1831, but finding it was
no simple task. After exploring Urchins' Kitchen, he climbed to
High Billinge, the highest point of the Delamere Hills. At the top
is a mound, covered by a copse of beech trees, which Coward
believed to be a Bronze Age barrow (he was later proved right).
Nearby, he met,

> an ancient inhabitant, much crippled with rheumatism, but
> withal cheerful and communicative. I ask him about Nixon
> and the Headless Cross. He had 'yeerd o' Nixon', but not
> of the Cross, 'Ask some of th'ould uns, it's a bit out o' my
> country.' Then a happy thought strikes him, and he grins with
> toothless gums. 'Theer's th' Edless Woman down at Duddon.'
> That was his own country; he knew the publics [pubs] there.
> When questioned further, he stops a passing farmer, an elderly
> man whom he calls a 'young feller.' The farmer can give no
> information, but suggests that it may be another name for the
> remains at Eddisbury.
>
> 'Oh, Yedsbury,' says my old friend, 'if it's by another name,
> so be it.' I leave him, gleefully chewing my tobacco, and cross a
> field to the top of High Billinge.
>
> 'Yo mun leave yer name on trees, theer's lots theer,' the old
> man calls as I cross the grass. He is right. Like so many other
> places, High Billinge is the repository for names of hundreds
> of fools who carve their own insignificant initials to sully the
> beauties of nature …

Like sandstone, the smooth bark of beeches encourages lovers to
enshrine their names, but I wonder if Coward realised how time-

honoured the practice is? In Roman times, sweethearts would do just the same and say: '*Crescunt illae, crescent amores*' (As these letters grow, so shall our love).

I visited the area 113 years later, only to find that 'Th' Edless Woman' had been demolished a few years earlier, so, with no hope of a drink, I went instead to see High Billinge.

The beeches, of course, have been steadily growing since Coward's day, and as the bark has expanded, so have those carved initials, stretching out to three or four times the size; faint, but still readable. Nature has had the last laugh!

And the Headless Cross? Coward found it in the end, and so may we. It sits at the side of the road in Longstone Lane, just off the A49 that, in medieval times, was the road to Vale Royal Abbey. It is easily missed, however, being not only headless but bodiless; a moss-covered stone – the base of the old cross. There is no sign of the shaft; nowhere for a blood-guzzling crow to perch. Further along the same lane is the Longstone, a broken shaft, but that is thought to belong to another monument altogether. Either or both may have been erected by monks from the Abbey as distance markers for the traveller and places for wayside prayer; they were a common feature of pre-Reformation England.

TUNNICLIFFE, BATES AND THE BEAUTY OF CHESHIRE

Ask people to name their favourite nature artist and a surprisingly large proportion will say, 'Charles Tunnicliffe!' Narrow it down to 'bird artist' and some will call him the greatest of all time, a tribute that would have made the modest artist squirm with embarrassment. Few illustrators, at any rate, have been more prolific, more popular or given more pleasure.

Even if you have not seen his engravings, scraperboards, oil and watercolour paintings, or his illustrations to the books of Henry Williamson, H.E. Bates, Ernest Hemingway, Ian Niall, Alison Uttley and many others, you are likely to have seen his work in Ladybird books and the cards that they used to give with Brooke Bond tea.

Tunnicliffe grew up in east Cheshire, and the scenes of his youth provided the raw material for his visual imagination. He explained this in one of his loveliest creations, *My Country Book* (1942):

> What urged me to draw and paint in the first place I cannot say; what is it which compels one man to be a farmer, another a wheelwright, and another a driver of trains? But what is certain is that my early environment, while not determining that I should be a draughtman or a painter, greatly influenced my work when I did begin to draw; in fact, it is almost safe to say that it decided its character, for I was born in a Cheshire village and lived and worked on a farm until I was nineteen. So you see, those years which are supposed to the most impressionable in one's life were spent in the heart of the country, in close contact with animals and birds, with farms and farmers and their ways of life, and with all the thousand and one jobs which the farmer has to do.

Between 1959 and 1961, he was asked to furnish ninety-six full-page paintings for the four books *What to Look for in Spring/Summer/Autumn/Winter*, to show children what they might observe in the countryside, covering many aspects of wildlife and farming. Charles drew on the old sketchbooks and memories of his youth for these scenes, which explains why, on first encountering them as a child, I felt so at home in those pages. Then again, anyone from lowland England would feel the same comforting familiarity, because the Cheshire Plain does not stand alone; it is an outlying portion of a much greater plain that covers the Midlands of England. Unlike the 'scenic' parts of Britain it is a man-made, productive landscape, one that is all too often damned with faint praise.

One man who chose, instead, to celebrate it was H.E. Bates. In his book *O More than Happy Countryman* (1943) – illustrated by Tunnicliffe, incidentally – he turned that view on its head, arguing that this utilitarian patchwork of handsomely proportioned farms, neat hedges, square fields, copses and winding lanes is the very foundation of the English countryside, the thing that makes England different from any other country in the world. The Highlands of Scotland are put in their place by the grandeur of Norway or Switzerland, but this landscape cannot be replicated anywhere:

> ... the only time I went to Cheshire I saw the Midland countryside repeated exactly in the Cheshire plain, and I got from it a sense of friendliness and comfort.

I cannot agree that Cheshire is an *exact* repeat of the midland pattern – here the fields are smaller, the hedges lower, and we

have a greater proliferation of narrow winding lanes, but the kinship is obvious.

This is the land that was imprinted on Tunnicliffe's memory and appears spontaneously in his artwork. But if you grew up in the Cheshire countryside and know his work, you don't need to be told that: the pictures have already whispered to your soul.

> Friends have often twitted me with being so fond of staying at home traipsing about Cheshire and Shropshire while I might be seeing Paris or Hamburg, or even New York and Chicago. They say foreign travel would improve my mind, give me broader views of life, and teach me many things; that it might cure me of the prejudices and the narrow-mindedness that make me prefer worn-out bits of sleepy old England to all the glories of foreign lands. My humble reply to all these vain deluders has been the melancholy remark that I have not seen all Cheshire, and I hope to see more of its fair lands before I die. (Fletcher Moss, 1913)

HEDGES AND FENCES

The 'sense of friendliness and comfort' that Bates felt is provided chiefly by the hedgerow, without which the English landscape would not be English. In April it is white and pink with damson, apple and blackthorn blossom; in May it gives us the heady scent of hawthorn flowers and creamy drifts of cow parsley; in summer, the dog rose, honeysuckle and elder flower; in autumn, blackberries and hazelnuts, and through it all, the song of whitethroats, linnets and yellowhammers.

That, of course, is not the reason for their existence; hedges are there to keep cattle in and intruders out. Moreover, they need regular attention: each bush must be persuaded to mesh with its neighbour when it would much prefer to shoot upwards, leaving gaps to either side. They should, therefore, be 'laid' every fifteen years or so, to keep them stock-proof.

As one might expect, different landscapes and types of farming have spawned a variety of regional styles. The Cheshire method results in a hedge about 3ft 6in high, tall enough to keep docile dairy cattle in but low enough to allow the hunt to leap over. As H.V. Lucas put it:

> Not high, but middle and low
> Is most of the Cheshire hedgerow,
> Enough for a bird to shelter in,
> Easy for life to toil and spin ...

Hedges are laid in the winter months while the hedge is asleep, and it is a solitary job, often done standing in a boggy ditch as an Arctic wind blows thorny branches into your face – you'll love it! My teacher was Jack Dunning, the hedge-laying champion from Waverton, near Chester, whose patience with beginners is as legendary as his skill.

After chopping out the old, dead 'stows' (stems) and cutting out the brambles, the first tree is cut near the base to more than halfway through; don't worry – so long as some sapwood remains the tree will live. Working left to right, each cut stem is lowered and laid at an angle with the others. The brush is laid towards the far side and trimmed to a width of 8 to 10in. The whole structure is stabilised by a single row of stakes placed 3ft apart. Finally, supple hazel branches called 'breelers' are used to bind the top of the hedge, although Jack simply tied the upper branches to the stakes with twine, as I remember.

It's one of those jobs that looks and sounds easy but, in fact, takes years of practice. If done well, new shoots will grow upwards through the laid hedge creating a dense mesh that birds

love to nest in. Your reward comes in the summer as you watch a brood of young yellowhammers take their first flight.

*

If you are driving home and, on reaching a crossroads, you see black and white metal railings replacing the hedgerows, you know, somehow, that you are inside the Cheshire border. Why? Because such railings are not, or rarely, to be found elsewhere. In 1929, the county council decided to replace stretches of hedge at road junctions with railings to give drivers better visibility. The top rail curves inwards, and they are usually painted black and white – as if the Friesian cattle and 'magpie' houses didn't make the landscape black and white enough. Since then, many have disappeared or been overwhelmed by aggressive hawthorns and blackthorns. Others, crumpled in road accidents, stand twisted and rusting, but some have been restored and repainted or replaced by new ones. They must have seemed obtrusive when they first appeared in the quiet country lanes, but now they bring a sense of local familiarity. Perhaps, far into the future, bands of enthusiasts will restore pylons with the same loving care.

MERES, POOLS AND FLASHES

'Of waters there are also great store, in manner of lakes, which they call meres.'

(King's Vale Royal, 1656)

Question: How many lakes are there in the Lake District?
Answer: One – Bassenthwaite Lake! All the rest are called meres, waters or tarns.

Cheshire, similarly, has very few lakes – Oulton Lake is the only sizeable one – but a wealth of beautiful meres, plus a number of pools and flashes.

The word 'mere', as one might guess, originally referred to the sea, or to an arm of the sea, but over the centuries it has come to mean a body of standing water. Another word for 'lake', then? Not quite. In the strictest definition, a mere is shallower in proportion to its size than a true lake. The bed is warmed and illuminated by the sun and aerated by currents, encouraging a rich variety and abundance of molluscs, flatworms and leeches, and allowing bottom-feeding fish to make a living. In a mere, the little waves gleam and cast rippling shadows over the backs of perch and bream.

In Cheshire, however, the name is also applied to deeper waters that began as holes made by gigantic blocks of ice, which were left behind by retreating glaciers and buried by sediments. The blocks eventually melted, causing the sediments to collapse, leaving these steep-sided depressions which later filled with water. They are called 'kettle holes', and our teapot-shaped county has plenty of them. In fact, Cheshire and north Shropshire form a sort of lake district of the lowlands, containing more than sixty waters of a hectare or more in size.

The queen of them all is Rostherne Mere, three-quarters of a mile long and 100ft deep, by far the deepest in the region. The village church is superbly placed on high ground overlooking the mere, and when its deep-toned bells are rung the sound echoes from bank to bank. Sometimes, you could swear that you heard the muffled tolling of another bell tolling in reply, but where is it? Below the surface of the mere, perhaps?

Some have thought so. One of the legends of Rostherne tells of an underground tunnel that connects the mere with the sea. Every year, on Easter Sunday, a mermaid swims up this tunnel and rings a bell that lies at the very bottom of the mere. And how, you may ask, did a bell get down there? Here's how …

Rostherne church needed to replace its old bell, and it was a joyful day for the vicar when he saw the shiny new one delivered. The new bell was bigger and heavier than he had expected, so he enlisted three strong labourers to haul it up the steep slope and bring it into the church. They tied a rope to the bell and, slowly and sweatily, dragged it along, but when it was halfway up, the thin rope snapped and the great bell clattered and clanged all the way down the hill to the shoreline, where it rolled to and fro, humming softly. 'Damn and blast the thing!' muttered Tom. The vicar frowned in disapproval but said nothing.

Harry knotted the rope and they started again. This time they managed to heave it a little further, but the knot was not

tight enough; it slipped, and down went the bell, even further this time, splashing into the water and coming to rest among the reeds and yellow irises. 'Oh, to hell with it!' shouted Tom, kicking at the ground in frustration. Dick went over to him and reminded him that the vicar was within earshot.

A stronger rope was found; one end was tied to the bell, the other Tom tied around his waist so that it could not slip out of his hands. The bell felt heavier now, as if it was sulking in response to the profane words. Moreover, it had an infuriating habit of rocking and swivelling from side to side, but after much hard work under the hot sun, the three men succeeded in edging it, inch by laborious inch, to the top of the incline – almost. At that point, the bell became snagged on a rock and refused to budge any further. Tom couldn't contain himself: 'Shift yourself, you **** ****!' He shouted at the top of his voice. At that instant, both Harry and Dick lost their footing and let go of the rope. The weight of the bell jerked Tom off his feet and dragged him down the bank as it hurtled towards the mere. Faster and faster it went until, with a resounding clang, it hit a tree stump and bounced into the air with poor Tom flying helplessly behind it. The other men watched in horror as the bell plunged into the middle of the mere and vanished beneath the surface. Tom splashed in after it and, with a desperate cry of anguish, was pulled down into the depths. Rostherne people have been careful about their language ever since.

An interesting story, but if it is true, we have to explain why an almost identical tale is told at Combermere, only 30 miles away!

Another story of Rostherne, true this time, tells of the shoals of smelt that used to live in the mere. Smelt belong in the sea, not freshwater, but Rostherne, uniquely among British meres, used to have a population of them. They were first mentioned in the late seventeenth century, but none have been seen since the 1920s; even a mermaid has to eat, I guess.

Industrial activities have added new meres to the collection. Shakerley Mere and the lakes at Newchurch Common, for instance, are flooded sand quarries. Landslips, caused by salt extraction, gave us others, like the Winsford Flashes. Others still were created quite deliberately to enhance the landscape, often by damming a brook: Lymm Dam and Tatton Mere were both born in this way.

Redesmere is man-made as well; it was flooded in the eighteenth century to serve as a feeder for the ornamental lakes in the grounds of Capesthorne Hall. It was a favourite haunt, in his younger days, of the artist Charles Tunnicliffe. Perhaps the reader has a copy of the old Ladybird book *What to Look for in Spring*? If so, turn to page 42. The picture captures a moment that the artist actually witnessed at Redesmere: a nesting coot sat quite unperturbed as a bream leapt out of the water in front of it. He also devoted a whole chapter of *My Country Book* (1942) to his favourite mere:

> Whether in the full-leaved dress of summer or the stark, bare gauntness of winter, it is ever beautiful and interesting, and is a place of which I shall never tire.

Young it may be, but Redesmere, nonetheless, has a legend all of its own. It once had an island that moved about from one part of the mere to another. An old folktale? No, the 'floating island' was marked as such on the 1842 Ordinance Survey map. It was a protruding part of the bank until, one wild winter night, a Siberian storm blew from the east across the countryside. All night it blew, spewing sleet and snow, battering down fences and wrenching trees from the earth. Such was its force that this chunk of the bank became dislodged and was blown out into the middle of the mere. On that night, the locals maintained, 'th'owd squire died'.

Only a few miles away, at Bagmere, there was a similar legend: whenever an heir to the Brereton estate died, great tree trunks would rise to the surface for a short time, then sink to the bottom again. The Breretons themselves used to put it down to coincidence but not the superstitious peasants. Nor did poets scoff at the idea; Sir Philip Sidney (1554–1586) included it in his poem 'The Seven Wonders of England', while Michael Drayton paid tribute in his *Poly-Olbion* (1612):

> That black, ominous mere accounted one of those that
>   England's Wonders make;
> of neighbours Blackmere named; of strangers, Brereton's Lake;
> whose property seems farre from reason's way to stand;
> for, neere before his death that's owner of the land,
> she sends up stocks of trees, that on the top doe float,
> by the which the world her first did for a wonder note.

No member of the gentry can die, it seems, without comment from a nearby mere.

Small meres once played a part in the linen industry. Bundles of flax were left to soak in the water so that the soft tissue could be removed. In Delamere Forest ('the Forest of the Meres') there is a 'Flaxmere' and a 'Linmere'.

PEAT MOSS (AND PETE MARSH)

If you go to Bagmere, hoping to see trees bobbing to the surface, you will be disappointed: the Breretons no longer live at Brereton Hall and Bagmere, though still marked on the map, was drained in the nineteenth century and is now just a swampy-looking field. A cause for regret? Perhaps, but we should remember that every shallow mere, however ancient, is slowly turning into something else. Generations of waterlilies die and their corpses make the water shallow enough for reeds to move in and create a swamp. After other plants gain a foothold, the swamp may turn into fen, or, as generations of sphagnum moss slowly decay, a peat moss. These mosslands are another speciality of Cheshire and north Shropshire. Some, like Black Lake, Abbots Moss and Wybunbury Moss, are 'quaking bogs': deep, glacial kettle holes in which the water is covered over with a floating blanket of moss and peat. They provide a home for all sorts of dragonflies, spiders and plants like the bog rosemary, bog asphodel, cotton grass and the sundew, which catches flies in its sticky tentacles and gobbles them up. It is not wise, by the way, to venture out onto a quaking bog; trampling can lead to the gradual disappearance of these species, not to mention the more sudden disappearance of the trampler.

In other places, like Danes Moss and Lindow Moss, the peat has built up to form a 'raised bog'. Many have been drained or dug up for fuel, but in the past they covered broad areas. Wirral is actually named after a plant that grows on peat bogs: bog myrtle, known to the Anglo–Saxons as 'wir'.

These raised bogs contain secrets, most of them not yet uncovered; things that, in other soils, would have mouldered to nothing centuries ago, but here are miraculously preserved. Listen to William Webb describing the Wirral mosses in about 1656:

> Moreover, in these mosses (especially in the black) are fir trees, found under the ground, (a thing marvellous!) in some places 6 foot deep, or more, and in some places not one foot; which trees are of a marvellous length, and straight, having certain small branches, boughs and roots at the one end, like as if they had been blown down with weather; and yet no man can tell that ever any such trees did grow there; nor yet, how they should come thither. Some hold opinion that they have lain there ever since Noah's Flood. These trees being found (which the owners do search out with a long spit of iron or such like) they are then

digged up, and first being sawed into short pieces very small, yea even as the back of a knife, the which they use instead of a candle to burn, and they give very good light.

Until the twentieth century, there were 'submerged forests' on the beach at Leasowe and Meols, which became minor tourist attractions. Trunks of oak and pine stood up to 3 or 4ft high, their long-dead roots still holding them fast in a stratum of peat, until the sea, which had revealed them, washed them away.

In 1983, however, Lindow Moss (near Wilmslow) threw up a thing even more marvellous! Two men who were cutting peat on the moss heard a bumping noise and looked up to see a human head bouncing along on their conveyor belt. They told the police, who promptly launched a murder investigation. A local man, who had strangled his wife and buried her in the peat more than twenty years earlier, realised that the game was up and confessed to the murder. Before he could be tried, however, carbon dating revealed that the lady had been in the peat not since the 1960s, but since the Roman period! The murderer was, nonetheless, convicted on the strength of his confession.

The following year, another head turned up at Lindow, male this time, and with its torso attached. Analysis showed that he too had been strangled, but his murderer made sure by also cutting his throat and bonking him on the head. This time, the murder community of Wilmslow had the sense to wait for the dating: probably during the first century AD (sighs of relief all round).

Pete Marsh, as he was soon christened, was, and is still, the best-preserved bog body ever found in Britain. He died a healthy man in his mid-twenties, with a trimmed beard, a moustache and sideburns and the well-manicured fingernails of one who was unaccustomed to manual labour. In his stomach, traces of his last meal were found: toast and cereal. There was also mistletoe pollen in his stomach, which shows that he was killed

in the spring. Apart from a fox-fur armband, he was naked.
Plenty of questions, few answers.

THE POND CAPITAL OF EUROPE

A visitor from the south of England once asked me, 'Why do
people sit about in the middle of fields here?'

'Do they?' I replied.

'Yes, I saw lots of them from the train.'

It was summer, the grass was high, and she was seeing the top
halves of anglers, sitting by ponds (or 'pits' as we call them) in
the fields.

> The traveller cannot fail to notice the large number of square
> pits in the green fields of Cheshire which are very different from
> the round drinking ponds of the southern shires.
>
> (Joseph C. Bridge, 1910)

Look at a map and you will see what he meant: there are blue blobs in every field, sometimes groups of two or three together, and most are not circular, but roughly rectangular, with rounded corners. The Cheshire Plain is believed to have the highest density of ponds in north-west Europe, about 86,000. Henry Holland, writing about the Cheshire meres back in 1808, made a more remarkable (if unprovable) claim:

> If to these natural lakes be added the artificial pieces of water, of which there are several extensive ones in the county; and the numerous marl pits which are to be met with on every farm; it may perhaps be stated as a fact, that a greater surface of land is covered in water in Cheshire, than in any other county in England, Cumberland and Westmorland only excepted.

Marl pits are the holes, now filled with water, that were dug by gangs of labourers in search of marl, a fertile kind of clay. The practice has a long history; *John Leland's Itinerary 1538–1543*, tells us:

> The chief reason and the original [origin] by likelihood of the manifold pools and lakes in Chestershire was by digging of marl for fatting the barren ground there to bear good corn. To which pits the fall of the waters thereabout and springs hath resorted, and besides the ground there being so deeply dyked there be many springs rising naturally in them.

Marling was not a recent tradition even in Leland's day; it can be traced back to the thirteenth century. Marl lies beneath the topsoil in pockets all over the Cheshire Plain. It is lime-rich, because it contains the crushed shells of molluscs from some ancient seabed, which, in a county with virtually no limestone, made it a valuable fertilizer. The farmer would throw it onto the fields and allow it to disintegrate before harrowing and then ploughing it in. Marl was used to give body to light, sandy soils, allowing it to retain water. According to an old rhyme:

> He who marls sand may buy the land;
> He that marl moss suffers no loss;
> He that marls clay throws all away.

An acre of land required about 100 tons of marl, and the benefit lasted for about a dozen years, before the marl began to sink.

The donkey work was done by nomadic gangs of labourers who had to dig down, sometimes as much as 20ft, to find the marl and load it into a cart. They were paid by the farmer or the local squire, but passers-by had to be wary, for the marlers might press them for 'lorgesse' (payment) as well. When money was given, the gaffer, or Lord of the Pit, would give a signal for the men to throw down their spades and picks and join hands. They then performed a strange dance and an even stranger chant. If the cash was less than 2s 6d (12.5p) they sang that they had received part of £500. If more, it was part of £5,000. The working day ended with drinks provided free by the employer. Egerton Leigh in his *Ballads and Legends of Cheshire*, wrote (perhaps based on aural tradition?) a Marler's Song:

> We are the boys to fey a pit,
> And then yoe good marl out of it
> For them who'd grow a good turmit.
> [Chorus]
> Who-whoop, Who-whoop, wo – o – o – o – o! [three times]'

… and so on for another eight verses. In a footnote, he says: 'I read the above lines to an old tenant, a marler of former days, as a marling song; and he said, "It's all reet, it's all reet, but au wonder au never heard that song before."'

By the mid-nineteenth century, better roads and canals made it possible to bring lime from Derbyshire and North Wales. Lime was a far better fertilizer, equally good for sandy, peaty or clay soils, and it led to a rapid improvement in Cheshire's agriculture. In 1845, William Palin wrote: 'Marling is now rarely practised. Till lately the shouts of marlers were to be heard on every fine summer evening, but now their whoops are seldom heard.'

And what of the pits they dug? You will notice that most are placed at the centre of a field, which was convenient for spreading the marl but most inconvenient for the modern farmer. Some, therefore, have been filled in and ploughed over, showing up only on aerial photographs. A few have even been used as cesspits, which gave Derek 'Blaster' Bates the idea for one of his funniest monologues: 'the Shower of Sh*t Over Cheshire'. Those that have been spared are going through the slow, natural process of succession that, over many centuries, will see them revert to dry land again. Some of the older or shallower pits have already dried out and become choked with reeds or willow and alder scrub, while others still have open water. A well-preserved example will be distinctly rectangular, and, like a swimming bath, will have a deep end (rounded) and a shallow end (square), where the cart was placed. Even today, the deep end may be steep-sided; indeed, in 1357, a woman drowned after falling into one at Cholmondeley, so be warned!

All that digging has made Cheshire a pondier place than most – the 'pond capital of Europe', some claim. Most of them have a resident moorhen, and often a reed bunting or sedge warbler (both known as 'pit sparrow' in Cheshire). This is also an exciting county for the lover of Anisoptera (dragonflies) and

Roger Stephens

Zygoptera (damselflies). Most of the British species are found here, and in better numbers than elsewhere. We must conserve these iridescent dandies, if only for their names; how could we say goodbye to the downy emerald, the azure damselfly or the beautiful demoiselle?

Not so pretty, but just as precious, is the great crested newt, becoming scarce across Europe, but finding a stronghold in our pits.

And in spring, when the newts mate underwater, the lilac flowers of lady's smock (*Cardamine pratensis*) dance on the banks. It won the vote to become Cheshire's county flower; an excellent choice, since one of its local names is 'milkmaids'.

Chester contains more than 650 listed buildings.

THE FIFTH PRETTIEST CITY IN EUROPE

Imagine a beauty contest among European cities. Which would get your vote? Paris? Rome? Florence? According to a 2013 poll of American tourists, none of those make it into the top ten. Venice? Yes, Venice scrapes in at ninth place, but leap-frogging all of them, in fifth place, is Chester. So, Americans would rather walk around Chester in a fine drizzle than lie in a gondola watching the sun go down behind St Mark's. Quite a compliment, and one that will stick in the craws of Bath, Oxford, Cambridge and York, none of whom were placed. Chester has been turning heads for centuries, which is why the other girls hate her. Here are a few excerpts from the many love letters she has received:

'With the odd ancientry of Chester we were much amused. It renders this city perfectly unique.' (Anna Seward, 1794)

'Chester pleases my fancy more than any town I ever saw.' (James Boswell, in a letter to Samuel Johnson, 1779)

'I must go again and again to Chester, for I suppose there is no more curious place in the world … It is a quite indescribable old town; and I feel, at last, as if I had had a glimpse of old England.' (Nathaniel Hawthorne, 1853)

'I have quite lost my heart to this charming creation, and there are so many things to be said about it that I hardly know where to begin.' (Henry James, 1872)

When driving towards Chester you begin to feel its charisma as soon as the cathedral appears above the treetops, and when you stand on the Eastgate looking west, the spectacle is almost overwhelming. Where else could you find such a riotous carnival of architectural fancy? And yet, there are those who are underwhelmed. Nikolaus Pevsner wrote:

'The result is gay – yes; it delights the eye in a country setting. But in the streets it jingles away too insistently. Still, the historical interest is undeniable … '

Others are less generous still. Chester, they say, is no more than an ostentatious Victorian confection, a pseudo-medieval toytown, a preposterous fake. This quarrel can be resolved; all we have to do is examine the buildings more closely.

We might start our virtual stroll at the Cathedral, a building that, inside, has examples of every period of building from its Romanesque north transept to its twenty-first-century song school. On the outside, the crisp detail of the sandstone carvings might arouse our suspicions. Look closely at those gargoyles and you may spot the faces of Benjamin Disraeli and William Ewart Gladstone …

Heading down St Werburgh Street, we find a picturesque row of timber houses on the left, but their Gothic decoration is machine-like in its regularity, and Queen Victoria looks down at us from one of the niches. The architect is the celebrated

John Douglas, who also designed the famous clock that crowns the Eastgate. On Eastgate Street, we find the same neatness in the black and white wooden frontages. None of them are older than 1850, whereas some of the brick façades belong to the eighteenth century.

So far, the 'fake city' brigade seems to be winning the argument, but we have yet to peel back the layers. In Eastgate Row North, squeezed on all sides by mock-Tudor skyscrapers, is a little pub called The Boot Inn. It boasts the date 1643 but its timber façade is as Victorian as any other on the street. Enter at row level, however, and you find yourself (when your eyes have adjusted to the darkness) in a long, low-ceilinged room that calls to mind the reaction of Henry James:

> Every stain and crevice seems to syllable some human record – a record of lives airless and unlighted … I am quite unable to think of them save as peopled by the victims of dismal old-world pains and fears. Human life, surely, packed away behind those impenetrable lattices of lead and bottle-glass, just above which the black outer beam marks the suffocating nearness of the ceiling, can have expanded into scant freedom and bloomed into small sweetness.

Upstairs, you will find an entire wall of original wattle and daub construction, indicating that the date 1643 is correct.

Opposite the Boot is a tall, Gothic-style stone building with a tower, known as Browns Crypt Buildings. It was built in 1858, which is why the carvings show little sign of weathering, but, as with the Boot, there is a surprise in store: enter the café at street level and you find yourself in a fourteenth-century stone undercroft with Gothic vaulting – the real thing this time. Chester has about twenty-five of these undercrofts (wrongly called 'crypts' by the locals), originally storehouses or workshops, and all built between 1270 and 1330.

We might wander down Watergate Street, narrower and far less showy than its neighbour to the east. Its timber buildings are dowdy, rarely photographed and generally outshone by their taller, younger neighbours, but they have better stories to tell. Leche House has retained its medieval Great Hall (open to the roof), its fourteenth-century undercroft, some fanciful Jacobean plasterwork and even a little eighteenth-century graffiti. Further down on the same side is Bishop Lloyd's Palace, built in the early seventeenth century and smothered in lively carvings. Across the road is a grand Georgian house called Booth Mansion. Inside, however, we find a picturesque muddle of stone arches and timber beams. The owner, George Booth, wanted to move with the times, so he knocked two medieval buildings together and cased them in brick. What an irony that, 150 years later, new brick buildings would be disguised behind wooden frontages! I could take you into other places – the Blue Bell, Stanley Palace, the Dutch Houses, the Falcon, Tudor House, the Olde King's Head, Gamul House, the Bear and Billet, – but I think the 'fake city' lobby has already conceded defeat.

The Victorians could have turned Chester into a museum. Instead they chose to blur the edges between history and fantasy to create a city like no other.

*

Nantwich people are proud to call themselves 'Dabbers', but ask them for the origin of the name and they all give a different answer! I have a suggestion: 'dab', in Cheshire dialect, means 'to give a blow' (e.g. *a dab i'th eye*). Could it be that Nantwich people were ready with their fists in times past?

MAGPIE HOUSES

The Mayor of Altrincham and the Mayor of Over;
The one a thatcher, the other a dauber.

Cheshire is a land dotted not only with black-and-white cattle, but also black-and-white houses: the county is 'par excellence the home of timber architecture' as the architect Edward Ould once put it. Old halls, churches, townhouses, taverns, mills, farms – even barns are often timber-framed, even if weatherboarding sometimes hides the construction. The best of them – the likes of Little Moreton Hall, Adlington Hall and Bramall Hall – are among the finest and best-preserved old timber buildings in existence.

A magpie's nest is strong enough to resist a force ten gale, and the same goes for a magpie house. The box-like frames of these buildings are held together with tried and tested joints, mainly the ancient mortice and tenon joint. How ancient? Well, it was used at Stonehenge to secure the horizontal lintels that link the standing stones. The gaps in the frame were filled by wattle: squares of basketwork made from bendy hazel switches, which slotted into holes in the beams. The daub was a cloying mixture of clay, chopped straw, animal dung (one hopes the Mayor of Over enjoyed his work), blood and hair, which was thrutched into the wattle to fill every cavity, then lime-washed or painted. If maintained, it should last for centuries.

In Cheshire, the structure was often seated on a sandstone plinth, which made it even more secure; so strong and flexible that a passing giant could pick one up and put it down somewhere else without doing it much harm.

When you next find yourself in the Alvanley area, perhaps walking the Sandstone Trail, look out for a beautiful old timber house, tucked away in the hills. The seventeenth-century

Austerson Old Hall looks like a natural part of the landscape, and yet I have seen an old photograph of that same building standing among flat fields near Nantwich!

That is because, in 1974, it was (no, not picked up by a giant!) dismantled, transported to Alvanley and reassembled in its present position.

Then there is the case of Dutton Hall. T.A. Coward's *Cheshire* (1932) devotes several pages to the architectural delights of this sixteenth-century hall in the village of Dutton, near Runcorn. Have you visited it yourself? If so, you were in Sussex, because, only a few years after Coward's book, it was bought by one Lord Dewar, who had it dismantled and re-erected as an extra wing to his home in East Grinstead. Neither of its two ghosts – one a Roman soldier, the other a mysterious, wraith-like figure – survived the journey.

Before shrieking with outrage at such desecration, we should remember that these halls may not have been created on the

The Wheatsheaf, Raby

spot; in those days, buildings were often supplied in kit form, ready to be assembled wherever the owner wanted them. Take a look at number 84 on Frodsham's Main Street and you will find Roman numerals carved into the beams, showing where they were to be jointed together, rather more easily than a shelving unit from IKEA.

Over the centuries, different styles of framing developed, all of which can be found in Cheshire.

Large framing can be seen in The Old King's Arms, Congleton, The Old Rectory, Mobberley and in some seventeenth-century cottages at Great Budworth. The vertical beams are wide-spaced, so the big, square panels often had to be strengthened by arching braces.

Close studding is a superior method in which the verticals are packed in more closely to make a sturdier and handsomer building. Gawsworth Old Rectory; the Chantry House, Bunbury; The White Lion, Congleton; and the Crown Hotel, Nantwich, are all good examples. Being costlier, both in wood and labour, close studding was reserved for high-status buildings, particularly townhouses. It was not unknown for the owners of large-framed houses to paint in a few extra beams to give them that prosperous, close-studded effect – they had mock-Tudor even in Tudor times!

About half of Cheshire's timber buildings are built another way – small framing – in which the panels are no more than 3ft square. Small framing emerged later in the medieval period as a poor man's alternative to close studding. It was used for cottages and barns, but sometimes for grander places, such as Handforth Hall and Churton Hall, both built in the 1560s. Many townhouses that present a close-studded frontage turn out to be small-framed at the sides and rear, like Sweet Briar Hall, Nantwich.

The regular panels produced by small framing just cry out to be doodled on, and builders, the Elizabethans in particular, could not resist the temptation to arrange their bracing timbers into a geometric design. The gentry of Cheshire and Lancashire took this decorative panelling further than anyone else, turning their grand halls into impressive showpieces.

Herringbone bracing, as seen at Gawsworth Hall, was a great local favourite. The pattern was sometimes reversed to form diamond patterns as at Little Moreton Hall. Another local fashion was coving, in which the eaves were covered up by curved, concave plasterwork; this too was then painted, often using the four-leaved clover motif that is peculiar to the region.

The overall effect was not always so jazzy, however; when first built, the timbers of these houses were a weathered grey, not sticky black, and the panels were painted in 'comely colours'. The effect was less dazzling than today, but more colourful.

The owners of such great halls also had townhouses, and these, too, were intended to impress the passer-by, especially in the seventeenth century. Take a look at Bishop Lloyd's Palace in Chester: clearly, the Bishop could afford to employ a team of carvers to smother the frontage in decorative images. Some of them are simply grotesque – like the moustachioed monkey-man hybrids who prop up the upper storey – but scrutinize the two coloured panels below the windows. With just a few symbols they tell you the owner's present position (bishop), his previous position (on the Isle of Man), and in which reign he lived (James I).

The Victorians turned all these colourful popinjays into magpies by whitewashing the panels and smothering the timbers with black tar to keep out the damp. Some have chastised them for it, arguing that the tar prevents the wood from breathing. The timbers were painted only on one face, however, and being already old and seasoned, their breathing days were, in any case, over. So it was tar, the same stuff that protected the fleet of Sir Francis Drake, that preserved Elizabethan halls such as Little Moreton and Bramall.

THE MAGNIFICENT SIX

Out of all these architectural delights I have selected six that are unmissable.

First out of the hat is Little Moreton (or Moreton Old) Hall, owned by the National Trust. So absurdly wonderful is this house that even Nikolaus Pevsner could not quite believe what he was seeing: 'Happily reeling, disorderly, but no offence meant – it seems at first unbelievable, and then a huge joke.'

To my eyes, it's like a house of cards (mostly clubs), teetering, ready to flutter down with the next gust of wind. Were it not for well-hidden crutches and struts, the place would have come crashing down long ago. The gallery at the top of the building buckles and sags under the weight of its gritstone tiles and, in its turn, oppresses the storeys below.

The oldest part of the house is the mid-fifteenth-century Great Hall, but additions were made until the early seventeenth. Polygonal bay windows encroach into the courtyard and nearly touch; on one is written:

THIS WINDOVS WHIRE MADE BY WILLIAM MORETON IN THE YEARE OF OURE LORDE MDLIX, and above another: RICHARDE DALE CARPEDER MADE THIES WINDOVS BY THE GRAC OF GOD.

When T. A. Coward visited in 1903, he was served tea by the caretaker – a Mrs Dale, who claimed descent from this 'carpeder'.

Bramall Hall (open to the public, under the management of Stockport Metropolitan Borough Council) is one of the most magnificent and best-preserved timber buildings in the country. The most beautiful room is the Withdrawing Room on the first floor, which bears the arms of Queen Elizabeth I over the fireplace, but the heart of the building lies below: the Great Hall, which is about two centuries older.

A romantic myth has it that an ancient right of way passes through the Great Hall itself, obliging the owners to provide food and entertainment for travellers. The council will be relieved to hear that no evidence for this right has ever been found. There was once a long gallery on the top, as at Moreton, but it became unsafe and was later dismantled.

Gawsworth Hall is such a desirable property that in 1712, two toffs, Lord Mohun and the Duke of Hamilton, fought a duel over it. The result was double defeat. The two men hacked at each other with swords until both lay dead!

It used to be notorious as a place where visitors were chased away with threats of prosecution for trespass, but the Richards family, who opened the house to the public in 1966, are much friendlier! Today, a visit to the hall can be followed by an evening of open-air theatre in the grounds.

> 'It is of other days that Gawsworth speaks. May the jerry builder never lay his vandal hands upon this place!' (Charles Tunnicliffe)

Adlington Hall, near Prestbury, became the home of the Legh family in the early fourteenth century. Today, seven centuries later, it can be visited by kind permission of – the Legh family! Once, it was a moated timber building arranged around a central courtyard, as at Moreton, but the south and west wings were rebuilt in brick in the mid-eighteenth century, giving it an interesting hybrid appearance. The other half is dominated by the medieval Great Hall with its impressive hammer-beam roof.

The organ was installed in the late seventeenth century and is considered one of the finest that survive from that period; so fine, in fact, that George Frederick Handel (a friend of the family) tinkled its ivories while visiting. As a gift, he set to music a hunting song written by Charles Legh himself – the manuscript, signed by the composer, is still kept at the hall.

The other two of our magnificent six are both timber-framed churches: St James and St Paul, Marton and St Oswald, Lower Peover. Both date from the fourteenth century or earlier and are believed to be the two oldest longitudinal wooden churches in Europe. Marton is distinguished by its curious tower with lean-to roofs on three of its sides. This church and the nearby Marton oak play an intriguing part in Alan Garner's novel *Strandloper* (see 'The Aborigine from Macclesfield').

The beautiful church at Lower Peover has a sixteenth-century stone tower, but the beams and plaster of the nave are two centuries older. The most famous object inside the building is an ancient chest, hacked out from an oak trunk, and fitted with four locks, the keys of which were held by four different churchwardens. Local tradition has it that, when a farmer chose a wife, the chest was unlocked and the wench challenged to flip the lid up with one hand. If she succeeded, she was judged to be strong enough for work in the dairy.

John Speed declared Cheshire lasses to be 'of a grace, feature and beautie, inferior unto none', but the farmer judged them by other criteria!

In the churchyard at St Oswald you may find a grave that has a bramble growing on it …

THE BRAMBLE MAN

John Byrne Leicester Warren (1835–95) was the last Baron de Tabley of Tabley Hall. He was a highly-rated poet, a close friend of Browning, and also Tennyson, who said of him, 'He is Faunus, he is a woodland creature.' Unfortunately, he was too sensitive to endure much criticism, which made him reclusive, and even caused him to lay down his pen for long periods. At one point in his life it was said that he had just two friends, one of whom had not seen him for five years, the other for six.

De Tabley was also an expert botanist, author of *The Flora of Cheshire* (1899) – the first flora of the county. He had a particular interest in brambles, which he cultivated in his own bramble garden at Tabley.

Now, brambles, as we all know, are easy to get physically tangled up in. In the past, country people often compared them to lawyers:

> 'What's the matter, Mester? Has a laryer gotten thi? We caw them sharp hooks, laryers, for if they clip thi by th'leg an' tha tumbles among 'em, it's God help thi.' (Fletcher Moss)

Botanists, on the other hand, become mentally tangled in brambles because different species have cross-bred to produce over 2,000 microspecies, identifiable only by the experienced eye. Those who attempt the brain-frazzling task are given a special name: 'batologists'.

Flowers often feature in De Tabley's poems, for example:

> When I am clear of human kind
> And slumber with the patient dead,
> Give me a fragment of regret,
> Bring me some silly wayside flower.

It seemed appropriate therefore, that after his death and burial in Lower Peover churchyard, the 'silly wayside flower' should be one of his favourite brambles. *Rubus laciniatus*, a species with deeply cut leaves and petals, was planted on the grave, and the grave-keeper was warned not to dig it up.

The gesture was wasted on some, as T.A. Coward discovered when he visited: 'As I stand looking at his grave some visitors come up. "Ah!" says one, pointing to the bramble that gracefully trails across the tomb. "See how the dead are forgotten! Even the brambles are allowed to grow!"'

Next time you visit Lower Peover (for every visitor returns sooner or later), look for the the tall cross that marks his grave and check the health of that bramble.

4

PRODUCE AND INDUSTRY

When Gerald of Wales visited Chester in the twelfth century, he saw cheeses that had been made by the Countess of Chester herself. Even more surprisingly, they were from milk given by her tame deer!

BLESSED ARE THE CHEESEMAKERS

Cheshire's importance as a dairy county has been noted from the early twelfth century onwards. Why, then, does the county not have its own distinctive breed of cattle like Hereford, Devon and Galloway? For centuries, our farmers kept all sorts of mongrel animals and laughed at the idea of selective breeding. The answer is simple: with such fertile ground, lush grass and mild winters, there was no need for it. A seventeenth-century visitor, Thomas Fuller, was surprised to see that Cheshire cattle were not housed over the winter as in other counties: 'It may appear strange that the hardiest kine should make the tenderest cheese.' The cheesemakers of Cheshire have, indeed, been blessed!

As agriculture intensified, the mongrels gave way to new breeds, such as shorthorns: a dual-purpose breed, good both for milk and for beef. Later, the black and white Friesians and Holsteins came into favour due to their higher milk yields.

Cheshire is, of course, home to Britain's oldest named cheese. So strong is the association that I still occasionally meet people who think (like the Elizabethan cartographer John Speed) that the name is a corruption of 'Cheese-shire'. In the past, many believed that the secret lay in what Fuller called the 'occult excellency' of the grass. William Camden wrote:

> The grass of this country has a peculiar good quality, so that they make great store of cheese, more agreeable and better relished than those of any other parts of the kingdom, even when they procure the same dairy women to make them … The grasse and fodder there is of that goodness and virtue that the cheeses bee made here in great number of a most pleasing and delicate taste, such as all England againe affordeth not the like; no, though the best dairy women otherwise and skilfullest in cheesemaking be had from hence. (Britannia, 1586)

Before our pastures were reseeded, one farm could produce cheeses that, although made in exactly the same way, had their own distinctive tastes. How? Different fields had different mixtures of wild flowers that gave the milk, and therefore the cheese, subtly different flavours.

Cheshire cheese was catapulted to fame in 1590 with an order from Queen Elizabeth's court, which wanted the best cheeses for the privy council's dinner. Thus, Cheshire became the first English cheese to be exported from its own region, and that brought new challenges. Farmers now had to produce different varieties, some to be eaten while young, others made to withstand the rigours of long-distance transportation. King's Vale Royal (1622) tells us:

> They make great store of cheese. In praise whereof I need not say much, seeing that it is well known that no other country in

the Realm may compare therewith, nor yet beyond the Seas; no, not Holland in goodness, although in quantity it far exceeds.

By 1650, huge quantities were being exported to London, and cheese-makers had to club together to satisfy the demand. Celia Fiennes, who rode between Nantwich and Chester in 1698, referred to this practice in her diary:

… what I wondered at was that tho' this shire is remarkable for a greate deale of great cheeses and dairys I did not see more than 20 or 30 cowes in a troope feeding, but on enquiry find the

custome of the country to joyn their milking together of a whole
village and so make their great cheeses.

Output quadrupled between 1680 and 1800 as the number
of cows grew and their yields were increased. Throughout the
Georgian period, Cheshire was the most popular cheese by far,
although much of it was harder in texture than we are used to
today. It came in three patriotic colours: red, the more traditional
white, and blue-veined. It was enjoyed in London's clubs, inns
and pubs such as Ye Olde Cheshire Cheese on Fleet Street, which
served coffee and cheese to the likes of Voltaire, Dr Johnson and,
later, Charles Dickens.

Pride eventually degenerated into swaggering one-upmanship.
A song printed in 1798 called 'The Cheshire Man' tells of a
Spaniard who boasts of the fertility of his native land and the
bountiful fruits that it gives forth. The Cheshire-born merchant
responds by showing him one of his cheeses, and replies:

> Your land produces twice a year
> Rich fruits and spice, you say,
> But what I in my hands do hold,
> Our land gives twice a day.

By the nineteenth century, that rate had been increased to four
or five times a day on many Cheshire farms.

After all those five-star reviews, it's time we had a rotten
tomato! George Borrow was not a fan of Cheshire cheese. In
1862, he stayed at the Pied Bull Inn in Northgate Street, Chester
and ordered:

ale and that which should always accompany it, cheese. 'The ale
I shall find bad,' said I; Chester ale had a villainous character in
the time of old Sion Tudor, who made a first rate englyn [a short

poem in Welsh] upon it, and it has scarcely improved since; 'but I shall have a treat in the cheese, Cheshire cheese has always been reckoned excellent, and now that I am in the capital of the cheese country, of course I shall have some of the very prime.' Well, the tea, loaf and butter made their appearance, and with them my cheese and ale. To my horror the cheese had much the appearance of soap of the commonest kind, which indeed I found it much resembled in taste, on putting a small portion into my mouth. 'Ah,' said I, after I had opened the window and ejected the half-masticated morsel into the street; 'those who wish to regale on good Cheshire cheese must not come to Chester, no more than those who wish to drink first-rate coffee must go to Mocha ... '

It is true, of course, that not all cheeses came up to scratch: by Borrow's time, London buyers were outbidding all others, with the result that much of the best Cheshire was eaten in the capital. Perhaps Borrow was fobbed off with a reject, or perhaps some of today's factory-made 'Cheshire' (i.e. a sweaty slab of curds, pressed together and shrink-wrapped in plastic before it has a chance to mature) had travelled back in time. If only Borrow could do the opposite and travel through time to the present, he would find the Pied Bull selling real ale and The Cheese Shop, almost opposite, selling real farmhouse Cheshire!

Having conquered Britain, Cheshire cheese rolled across the Channel into Europe. The French, not always generous in their opinion of English cuisine, nonetheless love 'le fromage Chester', even if they do get the name wrong. They have even written poems about it:

> *Dans le Chester sec et rose,*
> *A longues dents l'Anglais mord.*
> (Victor Meusy)

> (Into the Chester, dry and pink,
> The long teeth of the English sink.)

They also write songs about it. French composer Manuel Rosenthal wrote one called *La Souris d'Angleterre*, in which an English mouse travels to France and, once established in a house, foils all attempts to catch her in a trap. Every kind of cheese is tried: gruyere, brie ... At last, they try a morsel of 'le Chester' and her love for her native cheese seals her fate.

Since the nineteenth century the story is one of inexorable decline. People in the growing industrial cities and towns wanted their pint-a-day, and quick transport by rail made it possible to keep milk fresh. Many farmers, therefore, particularly in the north of the county, found it easier to sell their milk in liquid form rather than as cheese. This led to a southward slip in Cheshire cheese production. Stick the point of a compass into the map at Whitchurch, Shropshire (that's right – *Shropshire*!), and describe a circle with a radius of 20 miles. The circle covers the southern half of Cheshire, the northern half of Shropshire (essentially, an extension of the Cheshire Plain), and small parts of Flintshire, Denbighshire and Staffordshire. That area, roughly, was the heartland of Cheshire cheese in the early twentieth century.

Two world wars brought more disruption to the industry. Between 1914 and 1963, the number of farms making Cheshire dropped from 2,000 to thirty.

In the 1960s and '70s, Cheddar cheese proved more suited to modern pre-packing, and Cheshire, for the first time in its history, began to be out-sold. To make things worse, foreign cheeses – camembert, mozzarella, parmesan – began to muscle in on the British market. Today, the most famous cheese in England is produced on just four farms in the Malpas/Whitchurch area.

HOW CHESHIRE IS MADE

Milk is heated gently in vats, and a *starter* (a culture of bacteria) is added to turn it sour. Unlike the factory version, the milk is not pasteurised – it must contain friendly bacteria if it is to mature into a flavoursome cheese. Next, a complex of enzymes called *rennet* is added to the milk to separate it into curds and whey. A traditional source of rennet is the plant Lady's Bedstraw (*Galium verum*), also known, in Cheshire, as *Cheese Running*. The Elizabethan herbalist John Gerard, wrote about it in his Herbal:

> The people of Cheshire, especially about Namptwich where the best Cheese is made, do use it in their Rennet, esteeming greatly of that cheese above other made without it.

Gerard, you will have guessed, was a Nantwich man!

The curds are then turned on cheese tables to help to drain off the whey, which is often fed to pigs. The curds are then salted, chopped into small pieces, put into moulds, wrapped in cheese-cloth and squeezed in presses. After removal from the moulds they are stored to allow them to mature. The cheese can be sold after ten weeks, but, since the flavour develops with age, it is better when allowed to mature for longer. Red Cheshire has annatto added, which colours it orange and lends a slightly nuttier flavour, but the kind that attracts most connoisseurs is the least familiar: Old Cheshire Blue. This variety, after about five weeks of storage, is pierced with needles, allowing the air to penetrate and activate the mould, which grows into veins.

Compared to other cheeses, Cheshire is crumbly and relatively acidic, with a low calcium content, but since no two farmhouse cheeses are ever quite alike, the taste and texture vary. It should disintegrate in the mouth, and the taste should be clean, mild and milky with a salty tang as it goes down.

John Gerard

How can this endangered species be saved from extinction? The annual Nantwich Show helps to fly the flag with its International Cheese Awards – the most important cheese event in Britain. There are rumours that gourmets overseas are acquiring a taste for real calico-wrapped Cheshire, but the only way to ensure its survival is for us to eat the stuff. Seek it out. Pay a little more for it. There is no better cheese to sink your long, English teeth into.

In 1909, the dairy at Tattenhall Hall made a huge 300lb Cheshire cheese, which easily beat the previous record of 192lb, set in 1792. To prove it was no fluke, they went on to produce twenty of them!

DAMSON COUNTRY

> What a country this is for damsons! Not only are these typical
> Cheshire fruit-trees growing in orchards and gardens, but
> they line the hedgerows and border the roadside where every
> schoolboy can eat his fill. (T.A. Coward, *Picturesque Cheshire*,
> 1903)

Damsons are as widespread, as tasty and as scrumpable today
as they were in Coward's time, particularly in the south-western
half of the county where, in the back-end of the year, they add
a flush of indigo to the yellowing hedgerows. I speak, of course,
of the 'Cheshire' or 'Prune' damson, the most celebrated of the
county's fruit cultivars and the oldest and best variety.

Next to a plum, this small, oval fruit looks humble enough,
but good things come in small packages! Rub off the powdery
blue bloom and try it. The Cheshire damson is higher in sugars
than a plum, so its flavour is stronger and sharper.

Some trees are looked after, and their fruit harvested regularly;
others live in old, tangled, neglected orchards, where they
drop their dark fruits, unnoticed, into the long grass. Many
were planted randomly in hedgerows, close to farm buildings.
Damson can be a useful hedgerow tree, because its spiny
branches make it almost as stock-proof as its bitter-fruited
cousin, the blackthorn. Odd trees can be found even in the
loneliest lanes, often marking deserted settlements where, long
ago, squatters enclosed common land for their own use.

Chester used to hold a Damson Fair every year in late
September, where the year's crop was sold off to be made into
jam, pies, tarts, wine, damson cheese, damson gin ...

Damson gin is as easy to make as sloe gin and tastes even
better, so here is a recipe:

Collect 4lb of damsons, prick each with a fork (to allow the gin to infiltrate) and fill a large jar with them. Add 4lb of sugar and two bottles of the cheapest gin you can buy. Stir the mixture every day for the next 10 weeks or so until all the sugar is dissolved, then bottle it.

Damson gin is traditionally drunk at Christmas, but for a mellower flavour, wait a few months longer, perhaps until April, when you can toast the blossom that promises another crop next year. The Sale poet Hedley Lucas had a soft spot for it:

> When flowers the damson tree
> With blossom good to see,
> A Cheshire beauty's here,
> Five-petalled, white and clear.
> And as too soon is strown
> A bloom so lovely grown,
> Too quickly gone the light
> That gives a true delight,
> Around some Cheshire mile
> I make the most awhile
> Of damson trees that seem
> Like snowdrifts in a gleam.

APPLES AND PEARS

When John Wesley first visited Cheshire, he chose to preach, not at an obvious place like Chester or Stockport, but in the tiny hamlet of Alpraham. A sizeable crowd gathered around a pear tree at Moathouse Farm and there the great man addressed them. The year was 1749, and the visit left such an impression

that, when the tree breathed its last over a century later, another was planted in its place.

There are over 3,000 pear cultivars, but certain varieties, like the San Jam pear (also known as the green Chiswell pear) and the hazel (or hazzle) pear, have enjoyed a particular popularity in Cheshire. Altrincham's ancient San Jam Fair (which began in 1319 and was held every year until 1895) used to be held on St James' Day, 25 July. The San Jam pear was usually ripe by then, so it became a traditional part of the festivities.

Another forgotten tradition is Tarporley Races, which ran from 1776 to 1939. At this event the Tarporley peach was the favoured fruit – not a peach at all, but a pear, small, green and juicy. It is more properly called the hazel pear or Acton town pear, since it used to be grown in the villages of Acton Bridge and Crowton. 'Plant pears for your heirs' was a local saying. The trees are hard to find now, but the village still has a pub called the Hazel Pear.

More than thirty varieties of apple can be claimed for Cheshire. They have friendly, evocative names, like Chester Pippin, Bostock Orange, Lord Combermere, Elton Beauty, Moston Seedling, Chester Pearmain, Eccleston Pippin, etc. Minshull Crab is named after a famous tree that stood in Church Minshull in the eighteenth century.

One of the best is Lord Derby, a green, smooth-skinned, sharp-flavoured cooking apple first raised in Stockport in 1862. If you ever try your hand at baking Cheshire Fidget Pie (a traditional harvest-home feast, containing apples, streaky bacon and onions with Cheshire cheese added to the pastry) then Lord Derby will give it just the right tang.

THE GIANT GOOSEBERRY

> I met with Mr Looker, my Lord's gardener, who showed me
> … the gardens, such as I never saw in all my life; nor so good
> flowers, nor so great gooseberries, as big as nutmegs.
>
> (Samuel Pepys, 1661)

In Pepys' day, gooseberries were used mainly in savoury dishes; a tangy gooseberry sauce was found to be the perfect complement to roast goose, hence the name. They have never been popular eating on the Continent, however; in sunny climes they are dry, tasteless little things parched by the sun and thirsty for rain. If gooseberries are to grow fat and succulent they need some good old British weather; in fact, they thrive better in the north of England than the south. Moreover, the humblest amateur gardener, with enough patience and perseverance, can grow gooseberries to rival Mr Looker's.

Around the 1740s, growers in rural parts of the North and Midlands began to compete with one another and Giant Gooseberry Clubs were formed. By the early nineteenth century, Cheshire had become the centre of the gooseberry world; many villages had their own clubs, and shows were organised at public houses such as the Spread Eagle at Macclesfield and the Admiral Tollemache at Mottram in Longdendale. They designed and made special scales and calipers for the solemn task of weighing and measuring the competing berries. Apart from cash, prizes might come in the form of a pair of secateurs, a copper kettle, a cream jug, a pair of sugar tongs, or even a corner cupboard. The weights of the winning berries were published in the local papers and recorded for posterity in *The Gooseberry Book*.

Many growers, in their eagerness to trounce their rivals, became experts at selective breeding, and, in a relatively short time, produced hundreds of new varieties, each bearing bigger berries than the last. Even Charles Darwin sat up and took notice. In his 1868 book *The Variation of Animals and Plants under Domestication* he expresses astonishment at their achievement.

Little by little, as large-scale commercial growing of gooseberries got under way, the working man began to turn to other hobbies. Today, there are just nine gooseberry clubs in the whole of England and Wales, and all but one of them belong to villages within a few miles of the Jodrell Bank telescope (in fact, one local cultivar is actually called Jodrell Bank!). Those eight clubs comprise the Mid-Cheshire Gooseberry Association, the last refuge of the giant gooseberry in Britain. One of them is based in Goostrey, which derives its name from 'gorse tree', so its connection with gooseberry growing can only be put down to nominative determinism!

Only in the heart of Cheshire, it seems, do they still have the patience to nurture a bush through the four seasons of the year until it produces a berry the size of a hen's egg. Each club stages its own show in late July or early August, and awards prizes in the different colour categories (red, green, white and yellow) for the biggest single, double or triplet gooseberry (three monsters on the same stem). Size matters, of course, and in gooseberry growing it is *all* that matters. Even the growers themselves would not eat a prize-winner, knowing how many chemicals have been sprayed on it!

And the world record? That belongs to Kelvin Archer of Scholar Green, near Alsager: 64.49 grams.

Some of this produce gets a mention in the chorus of a song by Leslie Haworth, a fruit farmer from Kelsall:

Here's to Cheshire, here's to cheese,
Here's to the pear and apple trees,
And here's to the lovely strawberries,
Ding Dang Dong go the wedding bells.

THREE WICHES

Not so very long ago, only about 220 million years back, this part of the world was as hot and dry as the Sahara. The entire Cheshire Plain was made up of shallow salt marshes, where seawater flowed in and, due to the intense heat, quickly evaporated. Each tide left a new layer of sea salt, which built up and up to become the rock salt that, in mid-Cheshire, is always under our feet.

If you were to descend, like a miner, through one of the old shafts, you would have soil before your face for the first 30ft before reaching the first layer of rock. Ninety feet below that, you would meet the upper bed of rock salt, 70ft thick. Streaks of yellow, orange, red and brown show where sand blew across the salt marshes all those millions of years ago. After a brief return to rock, we come to the lower bed of rock salt, 120ft thick. Natural underground springs thread their way through these beds and bring brine up to the surface, where it can be evaporated in pans, leaving crystals of white salt.

When the Romans first ventured into the area they found a busy salt industry in the Weaver Valley, out of which three centres emerged: Northwich (called Condate – 'confluence' – by the Romans), Middlewich (called Salinae – 'The Salt Works') and Nantwich. Salt was one of life's essentials; without it, meat and fish could not be preserved through the winter – '*Sal est Vita*' (Salt is Life), as the motto of Northwich has it. These were the three wiches; formerly pronounced 'wyche' to distinguish them from unsalted towns such as Norwich or Ipswich. Their salt was transported all over the country (place names like Saltersford and Salterswall reveal the trade routes) and provided an income for landed families and religious houses across the county.

At this time, Nantwich, 'the greatest and fairest built town of all this shire after Chester', was well ahead of the other two, producing the whitest, purest salt. Welsh traders called the town Hellath Wen: 'the white salt-pit'. In its heyday, towards the end of the sixteenth century, there were 216 salt houses operating there, along the banks of the Weaver. William Camden visited, and described the process in his *Magna Britannica* (1580):

It hath one onely salt pitte, they call it the brine pitte, about some foureteene foote from the river, out of which they convey salt water by troughes of wood into houses adjoyning, wherein there stand little barrels pitched fast in the ground, which they fill with that water, and at the ringing of a bell they beginne to make fire under leades; whereof they have six in everie house, and therein seeth the said water. Then certaine women, they call them Wallers, with little wooden rakes fetch up the salt from the bothom and put it in baskets, they call them salt barowes, out of which the liquor runneth, and the pure salt remaineth.

Travelling on to the smaller works at Northwich, he noted:

… verie neere the broke of the river Dan there is a most plentifull and deepe brine pit, with staires made about it, by which they that draw water out of it in lether buckets ascend halfe naked into the troughes, and powre it thereinto, by which it is carried into the wich houses, about which there stand on everie side many stakes and piles of wood.

Northwich, however, was growing. It soon overtook its upstream rival and by the 1680s was producing three times as much salt as Nantwich. Success came at the price of pollution.

John Leland dismissed Northwich as 'a prati market town but foule', Celia Fiennes complained that 'the town is full of smoak from the salterns on all sides', while the Welsh knew it as Hellath Ddu: 'the black salt pit'.

In the year 1670, a fateful discovery was made. Coal, needed to fire the salt pans, had to be brought in from Lancashire, so the salt-makers, always looking for ways to cut their costs, ordered a search for coal seams nearer to home. They found something altogether more interesting.

As Celia Fiennes put it: 'they have within these few yeares found in their brine pitts a hard rocky salt that lookes cleer like sugar candy, and its taste shews it to be salt, they call this rock salt'.

The era of salt mining had begun.

A salt mine, unlike a coal mine, is a place fit for human habitation. Rather than tunnelling, the miners chipped outwards from the centre, creating a spacious, bell-shaped cavity in which the air was fresh and cool. Natural rock pillars were left standing, allowing the mine to grow larger and larger.

In the 1770s, intrepid visitors were lowered 300ft to the Dunkirk mine, to be awestruck by the 'immense solemn and awful temple'. The Adelaide mine attracted tourists – including Tsar Nicholas of Russia, who dined there with members of the Royal Society in 1844. The floor, walls and ceiling, lit by 10,000 candles, glittered to enchanting effect. Entire bands of musicians could be lowered, one at a time, in the bucket to play while visitors danced the night away. This mine covered 9½ acres, so several hundred people could dance together. No casual visitor to the blighted salt town of Northwich would have guessed that it had a magnificent concert hall 130ft below the surface – albeit with an unimpressive entrance.

All this was achieved by hard-working men wielding mattocks, a tool similar to a pickaxe, with an adze at one end of the head and a chisel edge at the other. A pair of crossed mattocks adorns the badge of Witton Albion, a football club that, when founded in 1887, drew its support from the mining community.

By the end of the eighteenth century, Northwich was the dominant 'wich', turning out 80 per cent of the Cheshire salt. For that, it could thank the Weaver Navigation, which left the town perfectly placed for bringing in coal and sending out salt. In Nantwich, the industry continued to decline and finally fizzled out in 1856.

It was around that time that the salt-makers had one of their worst ideas. They decided that, rather than paying men to hack away underground, it might be more economic to fill the old mines with hot water and pump it out as brine, a process known as 'wild brine pumping'. The water slowly dissolved the rock salt, causing the marl above it to collapse, with earth-shattering consequences for the town of Northwich, as we shall see. Did the industry sort the problem out or make reparations for the damage? No, it simply upped sticks and moved its operations to Winsford, where rock salt had been mined, in a small way, since the 1600s. By the late nineteenth century, Winsford had become the largest producer of salt in Britain.

Today, Cheshire produces fine salt for the table, brine for the chemical industry and rock salt for gritting icy roads. But which wich won the race in the end? Oddly enough, Middlewich, which has continued to produce salt from pre-Roman times up to the present day. More than half of all the table salt you have ever consumed came from this modest little town.

To learn more about the salt industry, visit the Workhouse Salt Museum in Northwich and the Lion Salt Works at nearby Marston.

The Winsford Rock Salt Mine opened in 1844 and is still working today, which makes it the oldest and the biggest salt mine in the world. Every year, it turns out a million tonnes of rock salt.

'SEE NORTHWICH AND DIE!'

Northwich has its uses other than as a salt cellar. Let there be appropriated to its service the injunction more familiar in association with the name of Naples. 'See Northwich and die'. The applicability of the rest of the phrase will become obvious if you have the temerity to remain after seeing.

(Ernest A. Bryant, 1901)

In coal mining towns people on the surface used to pity the men working far beneath their feet, breathing stifling fumes and living with the fear that the earth above their heads might collapse and bury them alive. In a salt town, where salt was both mined underground and boiled above ground, the situation was reversed. Here, the miners breathed clean air and worked in comparative safety. They felt sorry for the wretches far above them, who ingested toxic air and feared with every step that the earth beneath their feet might collapse and bury them alive.

It took a ton of coal to boil up 2 tons of salt, and the salt works used the cheapest, smokiest, lowest-grade coal they could buy. All over Northwich and Winsford, hundreds of short, squat chimneys coughed out sulphurous smoke as far as the eye could (or rather, couldn't) see. Steam rose from the brine pans and made an unholy alliance with the smoke to produce a suffocating, malodorous, mustard-coloured smog that irritated the eyes, oppressed the lungs and killed the grass for miles around. Travellers bypassed the town if they could. John Ruskin spent a lot of time at nearby Winnington Hall but kept well away from what he called the 'smoking hell hole'.

If the polluted air didn't shorten your life, employment at the salt works might. Here, there were no cushy jobs. Whether you were a fireman who tended the kilns, a waller who raked in and drained off the salt, a lumper who turned out the blocks of salt, or a lofter who stacked them up in the warehouse, it was all relentlessly strenuous work, mostly done in intense heat and exhausting humidity. The working day began at three in the morning and finished twelve or even sixteen hours later. For many workers, it was not worth going home after work was over. A factory inspector, in the 1880s, reported:

> The men, women and children were kept in the pan shed the
> life-long week, getting their meals as they could within the
> walls, and sleeping in some cavity which they had managed to
> hollow out in the neighbourhood of the furnace.

About 40 per cent of the workforce were women and children.
Another inspector drew attention to a possible moral concern:

> In *drawing* [i.e. taking the salt from the pan] the women wear
> a shift not always closely fastened at the neck and a petticoat.
> Often men are moving about the same pan, perfectly naked
> from the waist upwards. Owing to the heat and moisture,
> such clothes as are worn, instead of concealing, cling to and
> emphasize the figure. That is, when the mist lets you see any
> figure at all; for individuals are invisible to each other until they
> actually come into contact.

This poor visibility, together with the speed at which they had
to work, caused many deaths. If, while leaning over the pan to
rake the salt, you slipped and fell in, you were unlikely to survive
the scalding, even if fished out immediately. A government safety
committee recommended safety measures, but the salt-makers
contested them bitterly.

And there was a third way to die young in this town: the earth
might swallow you up!

Land can subside without the help of man, of course, especially
when it lies above salt deposits. In 1657, a 'dreadful and most
admired calamity' occurred close to Bickley Hall, near Malpas:

> ... trees did sinke downe with the earth into a water prepared
> to receive them underneath; the fall they made was hideous,
> representing thunder, or the roaring of a well-laden canon:-
> there come multitudes of people of all sorts, although in time

of harvest, to be spectatours of it. At the first they were afraid to come near it, but, one taking encouragement from another, some at last were perswaded to go to the brink and mouth of the hollow, and one or two were let down with ropes to see what they could discover: they were neither of them let down farr, but they importunately called to be plucked up again.

In Northwich, such calamities became an everyday occurrence. The first warning came as long ago as 1720, when a mine collapsed – the first of many. In those days, the lower salt bed was unknown, so mining was done relatively close to the surface, where water easily and inevitably dissolved the rock salt above mine workings and brine cavities. The earth shifted and wide crevasses appeared across roads or under canals, draining them of water. New lakes, called flashes, were added to the landscape.

Water could also find its way into mines where men were still working. They kept an ear cocked for 'Roaring Meg' – the sound of rushing water as an underground stream burst through – and, when they did, they ran for their lives. Pit ponies were quickly slaughtered on the spot to save them from the horror of drowning; they had been taken down as foals and were now too big to return to the surface.

The effects of subsidence on the buildings made Northwich a source of morbid fascination for many. Foreign writers advised their readers to come and gawp at the town as if it were a fairground freak show. One observed:

Some [buildings] overhang the street as much as two feet, whilst others lean on their neighbours and push them over. Chimney-stacks lean and become dangerous; whilst doors and windows refuse to open and close properly. Many panes of glass are broken in the windows; the walls exhibit cracks from the smallest size up to a width of three or four inches …

Many of the houses are bolted and tied together, but even then, they cannot be kept upright. This is not merely an odd case or here and there a house; but for sometimes twenty, sometimes fifty, and occasionally a hundred yards each way from the little valleys crossing the streets, the houses are affected in this manner.

One of my mother's most startling childhood memories was a visit to Northwich in about 1930. 'Now,' said her uncle, 'I'll show you what the salt industry does to a town,' and she became another wide-eyed subsidence tourist.

The Leicester Arms public house began to sink around the year 1830, but in a slow and dignified manner. Twenty years later, the customers were sitting in what used to be the bedrooms and the old tap room and sitting room now served as the cellars. The old Crown and Anchor on the High Street was rebuilt when the floor of the dining room had descended several feet below the level of the road outside and walking from one side of the room to the other was 'like being at sea in a heavy gale'.

By the end of the century, hundreds of buildings had been ruined: houses, shops, pubs, industrial premises, even the police station. Northwich people grew used to the fact that nothing was permanent, nothing could be taken for granted. A farmer left his horse in the stable and returned to find it had fallen down a 15ft hole. Another, leading his cow along the street, looked round to find it gone; his friend reassured him that sooner or later it would be pumped up with the brine and returned to him. A company of army volunteers marched from one side of the square to the other, then wheeled round to find that the ground they had just vacated was gaping to receive them.

People also became reconciled to paying for the damage and loss out of their own pockets. It was almost impossible to prove whose works was responsible, so the salt-makers would not agree to pay out. That finally changed in 1891, when the hotly contested Cheshire Salt Districts Compensation Bill was passed by Parliament, obliging each proprietor to contribute to a compensation fund.

The Cheshire Prophet Robert Nixon predicted that Northwich would be destroyed by water, and so it would have been, but for some technical ingenuity. The two slowly sinking bridges over the Weaver were replaced, in the 1890s, by new, electric-powered swing bridges that pivoted on a circular pontoon, independent of the shifting ground. Meanwhile, the architects were turning to the tried and tested methods of medieval builders. Brick and stone buildings were demolished and replaced by lighter timber structures. Some were 'brick-nogged', that is, the brickwork was held together by the wooden frame to prevent cracking. On more temperamental ground, they were built in wood throughout and decorated playfully in Tudor Revival style with carved figures. In the parts of town where angels feared to tread, light, single storey buildings appeared, so designed that they could easily be taken apart and moved. These were not even attached to their brick foundations; if the ground sagged beneath them, workmen could jack them up, fill in the cavity, add a few extra courses of bricks, and lower them down again. As Ernest A. Bryant put it:

> The town appears indebted to the hydraulic jack for its continuance upon the face of the globe. Out of many a hole this instrument has lifted them. Visitors are advised to carry several of these highly able instruments in each pocket.

Because of their strong construction, the new buildings could survive the most traumatic experiences. Castle Chambers toppled backwards into a hole and came to rest at an angle of 45 degrees, yet not one pane of glass was broken. The tightly screwed beams held the brickwork in place. The Wheat Sheaf Inn was rebuilt in timber and, year after year, sank and was raised up again, on one occasion, by 9ft. This yo-yo existence became routine, and of course, when the buildings were jacked up the street had to be raised up to the new level. Bridge House, which was situated on a particularly untrustworthy spot, solved its problem by moving further up the street. The whole building was jacked up, moved on wooden rollers back from the road, then behind some neighbouring buildings, and forwards again to a new location some 60 yards away.

These days, Northwich people sleep easier. The old mines have been filled with lime waste from the chemical works, and controlled brine pumping has replaced the old, irresponsible wild brine pumping. The only visible evidence of subsidence are the many flashes: lakes, large and small, which often have roads or canals passing across them. The Witton flashes (formerly known as 'the Ocean') cover a huge area just north of the town centre. Neumann's Flash and Ashton's Flash are both named after the owners of the collapsed mines that created them. In the mid-

twentieth century the chemical works used them as a dumping ground for lime waste, but today they attract birdwatchers and botanists. Ashton's has been invaded by lime-loving orchids; masses of fragrant, common spotted and southern marsh orchids turn the land pink during June and July. Neumann's is a tranquil lake, beloved of wildfowl and a winter haven for great flocks of gulls, lapwings and golden plovers.

On Ollershaw Lane, close to the Lion Salt Works, is a small pool where a pair of great crested grebes raises a brood every summer. In times of drought, however, when the water level is low, the lake gives us a sharp reminder of its origin: rusty remnants of machinery appear to rise, like Excalibur, from the depths. Why? Because the pool is directly above the famous Adelaide mine where, long ago, orchestras played, dancers danced and a Russian Tsar was entertained. The ceiling came crashing down in 1928.

In fact, most of the flashes are now as natural-looking and as full of life as the meres that trace their ancestry back to the last Ice Age. Perhaps the Northwich motto, *Sal est Vita*, makes sense after all.

FUN AND GAMES

THE LAST JESTER IN ENGLAND

If, on a visit to Gawsworth Hall, you take a stroll along Church Lane, you will soon come to a wooded crossroads. The road to your left bears the unappetising name of Maggoty Lane, and the wood, likewise, is called Maggoty's Wood. Explore the wood and you will soon find a curious grave, consisting of two engraved slabs. Underneath, long since picked clean by maggots, lie the bones of Samuel Johnson.

Yes, I know: the great writer and lexicographer is buried in Westminster Abbey, but this is the resting place of Cheshire's Samuel Johnson, born in 1691, eighteen years before his namesake. Samuel 'Maggoty' Johnson was not only a writer, but also an actor, a poet, a fiddler, a dancing master, a stilt-walker and a wit. In 1729, he was the toast of London's West End, yet, today, he merits only half a page in the Gawsworth Hall guidebook. What went wrong?

The Haymarket Theatre was nine years old when it enjoyed its first great success: a nonsense play with music called *Hurlothrumbo, or the Supernatural*, put on by a bunch of unknowns from Cheshire and Manchester. It played to packed houses for thirty nights or more – an exceptionally long run for the time – and turned its author, Samuel Johnson, into a celebrity overnight. After the fifteenth performance, Johnson found himself dining with the likes of the Duke of Montague, Lord Walpole and the Duchess of Bedford. A Hurlothrumbo Society was founded by his admirers.

Johnson's northern friends were employed as 'claqueurs': their job was to sit in the audience, laugh at all the jokes and applaud wildly at the end of each act. One of them, the poet John Byrom, wrote of the play's 'oddities, flights, comicalities, madness and whimsicalities', and noted:

> Mr Johnson ... is the chief topic of talk in London. Dick's Coffee-house resounds 'Hurlothrumbo' from one end to the other ... They say the Prince of Wales has been told of 'H' and will come and see it ... For my own part, who think all stage plays stuff and nonsense, I consider this a joke upon them all.

It is all the more surprising, therefore, to find that posterity has taken a very different view:

> A more curious or a more insane production has seldom issued from human pen.
>
> (F. Lawrence, 1855)

> Perhaps unrivalled in the English language for absurd bombast and turgid nonsense.
>
> (J.P. Earwaker, 1854–57)

Let us take a look at the first edition and judge for ourselves. On the title page, Johnson writes:

> Ye sons of fire, read my Hurlothrumbo,
> Turn it betwixt your finger and your thumbo,
> And being quite undone, be quite struck dumbo.

Cheshire Rounds - a dance tune from Maggoty's day

No setting or period of history is specified, but we appear to be in a vague, fluid world of classical mythology, fantasy and magic in which anything can happen. The characters (sixteen male, five female) have names like Soarethereal, Dologodelmo, Urlandenny and Lomperhomok. Some of them rise in rebellion against the king, who is betrayed by his own champion, Hurlothrumbo, but the rebels are defeated, the champion forgiven, and that, give or take a few love triangles, is the plot.

Johnson wrote a part for himself, of course: Lord Flame, a babbling madman who seems to have little to do with the story but gave the author a chance to display his multifarious talents: dancing, singing, fiddling and teetering about on stilts. There was spectacle, too; one stage direction reads: 'A genius [guardian spirit] descends in a cloud, and Death enters upon a pale-dun horse.'

A year earlier, John Gay's *Beggar's Opera* had enjoyed a comparable success by ridiculing Italian opera, but Johnson's show was wilder, more surreal, mixing the sublime with the vulgar, satire with nonsense. Here, for example, is the king planning to make his troops drink brandy laced with gunpowder:

Then lightning from the nostrils flies,
Swift thunder-bolts from anus, and the mouth will break,
With sounds to pierce the skies, and make the earth to quake.

There are moments of inspired satire, but they are separated by pages of loquacious nonsense that leave the modern reader not so much struck dumbo as mentally numbo.

Byrom contributed an epilogue, which consists of a dialogue between the Author and a Critic, giving Johnson an opportunity to defend his creation before the real critics descended:

Cr: I say, sir, rules are not observed here –
Au: Rules, like clocks and watches, were all made for fools.
Rules make a play? That is –
Cr: What, Mr. Singer?
Au: As if a knife and fork should make a finger.
Cr: Pray, sir, which is the hero of your play?
Au: Hero? Why, they're all heroes in their way.
Cr: Why, here's no plot! – or none that's understood.
Au: There's a rebellion, tho'; and that's as good.
Cr: No spirit nor genius in't.
Au: Why didn't here
A SPIRIT and a GENIUS both appear?
Cr: Poh, 'tis all stuff and nonsense –
Au: Lack a day!
Why that's the very essence of a play.
Your old-house, new-house, opera and ball;
'Tis NONSENSE, critic, that supports 'em all.
As you yourselves ingeniously have shown,
Whilst on their nonsense you have built your own …

Johnson's standard reply to criticism of the work was to declare that he wrote the entire thing holding a fiddle in his other hand, and that readers should do likewise if they wished to appreciate it fully.

Rival authors looked on with mingled astonishment, envy and bitterness. The young Henry Fielding, whose early plays had met with rejection by London theatres, planned revenge on the northern upstart and, within a year, got his opportunity. His comedy *The Author's Farce*, which opened at the very same theatre, lampoons the London theatre scene for its reliance on novelty and empty frivolity. One character declares:

> If you must write, write nonsense, write operas, write entertainments, write *Hurlothrumbos*, set up an oratory and preach nonsense, and you may meet with encouragement enough.

Johnson was undeterred. The following year, his *Chester Comics* was staged, and over the next decade, a succession of comedies, operas and farces. Friends of Dr Samuel Johnson heard of them and feared that they might be misattributed to the great man. However, each of these shows made less impression than the last, and the author knew just as well as his namesake that 'no man but a blockhead ever wrote, except for money'. The strain was beginning to tell as well: at the opening night of his *All Alive and Merry*, Samuel's own merriness led to unseemly fisticuffs in the pit. It was time to go back home.

Samuel spent the last thirty years of his life in his native county, relying on the generosity of wealthy patrons. The Earl of Harrington, owner of Gawsworth Hall, appointed him dancing master to his children, and he was granted lodging in the New Hall with a servant all to himself. His brilliant wit and excellence on the fiddle ('Fiddler Johnson' was one of his nicknames) were renowned; he was invited to visit other houses in the area and many called by at Gawsworth to be entertained. He became, in effect, a paid jester, perhaps the last of that ancient profession.

What sort of man was he? His self-portrait (as well as his fiddle) adorns a wall inside the old hall and he looks so much like Gene Wilder that one wonders if there is a genetic link. The face is proud, refined and full of intelligence; the face of a wit, not a clown.

The character of Lord Flame (reincarnated in a later play as Lord Wildfire) entered his soul and he insisted on the title to the end of his life. Many called him 'My Lord' to his face and, behind his back, 'Old Maggoty', which, in those days, meant 'whimsical' or 'capricious'. His behaviour could be reckless and eccentric; he once terrified a nervous old lady by politely assuring her that, after his death, he would do her the honour of haunting her first. He found a false friend in alcohol, and after one particularly spectacular bout of drunken behaviour, woke up to find himself in the stocks. The irony was that he had been put there by fellow actors who were visiting Gawsworth. The shame of that episode made him reclusive; in a letter to a friend he confided that he would have to retreat from his beloved Gawsworth and leave no trace behind.

He never lost faith in his own genius, however. A year or two before his death, he wrote:

> I heard the Duke of Montague say, that if Homer was in London in this age, and did write for the play-house, his genius would be thrown away; for the masters would not do his work the honour to look at it. I have made five operas, and all of them were performed in public; but then I was young and acted in them myself; but now I am about fourscore years old, and cannot act any more; but as this opera is much the best that ever I made, I am desirous to see it performed before I leave the world.

He made careful arrangements for his funeral. He would not contemplate burial in the churchyard, because he feared that, at the Resurrection, some old crone buried nearby might argue with him about which leg bone belonged to whom. Therefore, the last jester in England found a secluded resting place surrounded by whispering trees.

Both of the stones are engraved with verses, those on the lower slab being a moralising admonishment of Maggoty written by the local curate in 1851. I suggest that you ignore them and read instead the epitaph that he wrote for himself:

Under this stone rest the remains of Mr Samuel Johnson
Afterwards ennobled with the grander title of
Lord Flame
Who after having been in his life distinct from other men
By the eccentricities of his genius
Chose to retain the same character after his death
And was, at his own desire, buried here May 5th
A.D. MDCCLXXIII aged 82.
'Stay, thou whom chance directs or ease persuades,
To seek the quiet of these sylvan shades.'
Here, undisturbed and hid from vulgar eyes,
A wit, musician, poet, player, lies
A dancing master too in grace he shone,
And all the arts of opera were his own,
In comedy well skilled he drew Lord Flame,
Acted the part and gaind himself the name,
Averse to strife how oft he'd gravely say,
These peaceful groves should shade his breathless clay,
That, when he rose again, laid here alone,
No friend and he should quarrel for a bone,
Thinking that were some old lame gossip nigh,
She possibly might take his leg or thigh.

I hardly need add that Samuel's ghost has been seen many times, wandering these woods.

THE JESTER FROM SANDBACH

A Halifax bomber pilot in the Second World War, a bomb disposal expert, a demolition man who carried sticks of gelignite around in his pocket, a stunt motorcyclist who performed the wall of death – such a man has no right to live to the age of 83!

Then again, Derek Mackintosh Bates did nothing by halves. Born in Crewe in 1928, he was always larger than life – 6ft 4in in his socks.

When the war ended, he found that his old employers at Rolls-Royce had no job for him, so he adapted his wartime skills and became a freelance demolition and explosives expert. He later observed: 'Over the years I've managed to do all right while they've gone steadily bust!'

'Blaster' Bates earned his nickname by demolishing the landscape of L.S. Lowry; relieving the north-west of England of its obsolete factory 'chimbleys' – 500 of them over a long career. The name would have been forgotten, however, had he not discovered an additional talent: when asked to give a talk about his work he found that he could quickly detonate an audience into explosions of laughter. Before long, he had made his first recording, which led to more, then TV chat shows and one-man shows all over the country.

Bates was an effortless comedian with a parrot's ability to mimic the vernacular of old Cheshire farmers or the rarified tones of the Wilmslow and Alderley Edge Ladies' Luncheon Club. In stories like 'The Naming of Knicker Brook', 'The Pub that Changed Colour' and 'The Shower of Sh*t' over Cheshire, he indulged in vocabulary that would be considered fruity even today. It was a robust, uninhibited, irreverent brand of humour that, in our age, would come under political scrutiny:

> I've brought some of the gelignite with me; you notice it's very much like marzipan. Just the job for the mother-in-law's birthday cake – you get her to light the candle and you piddle off out quick!

It was a freer, less sensitive age, of course. Batesy was talking to his own people; he was one of them and they laughed openly and joyously. He was a naturally funny man, and he never failed to have his audience rolling about in joyful pain within minutes.

There is something else that would not be allowed today: Blaster carried sticks of 'jelly' about in his pocket. He would sometimes fish one out, light the fuse and leave it to fizz away while he told his story, snuffing it out in the nick of time. He once produced one while giving evidence in a courtroom, creating panic amongst the jury: he forgot to tell them that explosives are harmless without a detonator.

For all the national fame, Blaster continued working and stayed in his home town of Sandbach, so there were always new stories to tell.

Another great jester; let us hope he is not the last of his kind in England.

The radio comedy *Stockport, so Good they Named it Once* was first aired in 1999. This opinion was proved true in 2013, when the town was voted the second happiest place to live in Britain.

THE OLDEST BRASS BAND IN THE WORLD

The brass band is a great nineteenth-century working-class tradition. As heavy industries sprang up and smoky towns grew around them, so did the bands. Like football clubs, they were more than a pastime: they helped to bind these new communities together.

They are, of course, still bound up with the industries, especially collieries, that used to sponsor them, so some find it hard to dissociate them from belching chimneys, knocker-uppers, tripe and onions, and the slow movement of Dvorak's *Opus 95*. Brass bands are regarded as homely, local, amateurish, pom pom pom, a source of nostalgia, perhaps, but left behind by the modern world.

That view was not shared by Elgar, Vaughan Williams, Holst, Malcolm Arnold or Harrison Birtwistle. They, and a host of other leading composers, including the Cheshire-born John Ireland, all wrote brass band music because they recognised that many of these amateur ensembles had reached the highest level of virtuosity. So, if great composers respected them, why does the general public look down its nose?

British bands are ranked in 'sections', which are similar to leagues in football. The Championship Section holds the top ten bands in Britain, and it includes two Cheshire bands. To put that in footie terms, imagine that Chester City, Stockport County, Crewe Alexandra and Tranmere Rovers were all leading members of the Premier League. In the world of brass bands, two titles are coveted by all: the 'Open' (British Open Brass Band Championships) and the 'National' (National Championships of Great Britain). To win both is like winning the league and Cup double, and in 2012, a band from Sandbach did exactly that!

Had it not been for the relief of Mafeking in 1900, Fodens Band might never have existed. When the good news came through, the village of Elworth wanted to celebrate by inviting several bands from the Sandbach area, including the Wheelock Temperance Band, to march over and provide patriotic music for the celebrations. Unfortunately, one of the Sandbach pubs was offering free beer for band members, with the result that nobody turned up. Snubbed, and disgusted by such apathy, the worthies of Elworth formed a band of their own, which, after a few years, was revitalised by Edwin Foden of the local Steam Wagon Works. By 1908, it had achieved Championship Section status, a position that it has never lost. Over the years, it has won the National thirteen times, the Open twelve times, and played for several Royal Command performances.

As the band rose higher and higher, however, the motor works sank lower and lower, and, in 1980, was swallowed by a bigger fish.

The Fodens Band has a serious rival on its doorstep: the Fairey Band from Stockport. It was founded in 1938 at the Fairey Aviation works, and, like Fodens, is one of the top ten bands in the country. The Fairey has captured nine National titles, fifteen Opens and won the double several times.

Both bands play difficult music with dazzling virtuosity, and both, coincidentally, have been conducted by the legendary Harry Mortimer. Look hard at the map of Sandbach and you will find a 'Harry Mortimer Way' – the town has shown its gratitude.

None of this should surprise us, because the brass band tradition actually *began* in Cheshire! The Stalybridge Old Band was established in 1809 and is claimed to be the first civilian brass band in the world.

One of their early gigs was an opportunity to perform at a political rally in St Peter's Square, Manchester, on 16 August 1819. The speaker, Henry Hunt, was a fan of the band, so they were asked to play some music while the crowd of 60–80,000 settled down. Having done their turn, the musicians retired to a house in Ancoats for some well-earned refreshments. It was some time before they heard that the meeting had turned into the bloodbath that we now remember as the Peterloo Massacre, in which fifteen were killed and 400–700 were injured. Slipping out through the back door, the bandsmen made their way quickly and quietly through the back streets and returned home unscathed.

The Stalybridge band, in those early days, contained an interesting, eclectic mix of instruments: flutes and clarinets played the melody line, accompanied by natural trumpets, a serpent and an ophicleide. It was not until the 1940s, by which time the valve cornet had been invented, that it began to resemble a brass band as we know it.

The Stalybridge Old Band may not play with the brilliance of the Fairey or the Fodens, but, after more than 200 years, it is still going and still playing! Yes, a great working-class achievement; one in which Britain, and Cheshire in particular, could take more pride.

CHAMPIONS OF THE WORLD

No Cheshire town has ever had to cordon off its streets so that the FA Cup could be paraded in an open-top bus, but there is one town that knows the glory of being World Champions. Well, not exactly a town – Bosley has a population of 406 – but it has, on two occasions, carried off a world title for tug of war!

It all began in 1947 when some young farmers formed a club and adopted the toughest training method they could think of: with the help of a stout oak tree and a pulley system, they pulled against eighteen milk churns filled with sand. Before long, they were churning up the mud at agricultural shows and pulling all their opponents headlong into it.

In 1957, a local firm, Wood Treatment Ltd, stepped in as sponsors, and the team adopted the uninspiring but soon to be famous name 'Wood Treatment Bosley'. Onward and upward! Starting in 1959, they won the AAA outdoor tug of war championship (catchweight) for twenty consecutive years. They have also won nine European titles and two world titles in 1975 and 1976.

It proves the truth of the old saying:

Cheshire born, Cheshire bred,
Strong i' th' arm and weak …

I forget how it ends.

There is another Bosley on the other side of Cheshire, but the name is spelt 'Burwardsley'. Nearby Chumley is spelt 'Cholmondeley'. So, why is Plumley not spelt 'Plolmondeley'?

BLUE CAP

If you have ever used the A556, you will be familiar with the Blue Cap at Sandiway, the white-walled pub that sits at an angle to the road, behind a more than generous car park. Inside, they have old photographs of the building when that same space was milling with hounds, while ladies and gentlemen sat in the saddle, enjoying a stirrup cup before setting off to hunt the fox. Their coats were scarlet, no doubt, but whoever heard of a huntsman wearing a blue cap? No, the pub sign makes it clear that Blue Cap is a foxhound, and a famous one at that. Until recently, there was a model of him atop a column by the roadside, standing as proudly as Nelson; when I last called, he had been stowed away in a corner of the pub.

Blue Cap

In 1763, the year when he was rocketed to stardom, Blue Cap was a 4-year-old hound belonging to the Hon. John Smith-Barry of Marbury Hall, whose pack was kennelled nearby. The quality that marked him out from the pack was his speed. When the hunt was on, he had to carry a weight around his neck to allow the rest of the pack to keep up with him.

It so happened that Smith-Barry was a friend and rival of Hugo Meynell, the Master of the famous Quorn Hunt in Leicestershire, who had been breeding some fleet-footed hounds himself. Smith-Barry challenged him to a race between two dogs of his and two of Meynell's. The two men staked 500 guineas (£100,000 today) on the race, while other supporters on either side made bets of their own.

> They talk of Hugo Meynell and what he can do;
> We'll ride 'em and beat 'em, this Leicestershire crew.
> We've maybe forgotten a lot that they knew,
> And we'll teach 'em, Eh, ho!
> How the Cheshire can go!

The grand event was held at Newmarket Heath in Suffolk, on the site of the modern racecourse, on 30 September 1763. The four dogs were to follow a scent over a 4-mile course. Smith-Barry chose Blue Cap, naturally, as his first racer. His daughter, Wanton, was a bit of a goer as well (Blue Cap's daughter, I mean, not Smith-Barry's), so she lined up alongside him as the second Cheshire dog. Meynell's hounds were favourites at 7–4.

Off they went: four hounds, together with about sixty humans following on horseback …

The whole affair was decided in less than ten minutes. Our hero Blue Cap was the first to cross the tape, closely followed by Wanton. The first Quorn dog was 100 yards behind, and the other lost its way and never completed the course. Blue Cap's time was a few seconds over eight minutes: an average speed of 30mph.

Cheshire had defeated Leicestershire, and Blue Cap's achievement would be crowed from the rooftops for generations after. If, when taken out for his daily exercise, he was led past a village school, the boys would leave their books and rush out to feed him with bits of bread. One of them, in his old age, said, 'We viewed him with as much veneration as Wellington or Blucher in after-years.'

His portrait was painted at least twice. One of them still hangs on a wall in the Swan, Tarporley, and a handsome hound he looks – mostly white with a few smudges of black and tan. And, of course, a pub called the Sandiway Head has been known ever since as The Blue Cap Hotel.

The dog enjoyed his celebrity status for another nine years. After his demise, a very grand stone monument was built, which is now set up at the Sandiway Kennels: a sandstone obelisk, over 6ft high, on a plinth surrounded by a low wall and railings. On one face a brass plaque carries a poem written in his honour. How many dogs are commemorated by a Grade II listed building?

In 1867, the poet Egerton Leigh offered a poetical tribute, in the form of a double acrostic:

> Bluecap's remains, his dust and Bone
> Lie amidst that meadow green and Lone
> Untired in speed he won his Urn
> E'en harder than most heroes Earn
> Cheshire will never foxhound Call
> Amongst her pack that betters All
> Perfection write on Bluecap's Pall.

In a sense, Blue Cap is still with us, because research into pedigree suggests that some of his blood runs in the veins of every modern foxhound!

The first horse race on the Roodee course, Chester, took place in 1539, which many believe makes it the oldest, continuously used racecourse in Britain. It is also the most beautiful, cradled by the medieval wall and a loop of the river Dee.

FIG PIE ROLLING

At Wybunbury (pronounced 'Wimbury'), not far from Nantwich, they have a tradition that seems to be peculiar to the village. Every June, at their Wakes Festival, crowds of more than a thousand gather outside the Swan Inn to watch as fig pies are rolled along the road. I'm serious.

The locals claim a 200-year-old history for their custom. A poster dated 1819 proves that it was a fixture of Wakes Week at that time, but, as so often when alcohol is freely available, rivalries led to drunken brawls and the practice was banned. Football is not the only major sport to have been plagued by hooliganism.

In 1995, however, fig-pie-rolling rose like a phoenix from the ashes; old recipes were rediscovered, the art of baking the pies was revived and competitors began to hone their rolling skills.

The secret, as you may have guessed, lies in the pastry, which has to be harder than millstone grit if the pie is to whizz down the hill at speed. It is made from salt dough: one cup of flour to two cups of salt. If the pie is too soft, it will disintegrate after a few yards and be, deservedly, trodden on; if it is not balanced or skilfully spun it will veer off course and disappear down a grid. Such is the fate of inferior pies. For the pie that travels the furthest, however, there is undying glory.

The winning pie is cut open by the judges to check that it contains only figs and apples and is not reinforced by a hubcap or a wheel from an old pushchair.

Could anything be sillier than that? Surely not …

WORM CHARMING

At nearby Willaston (pronounced 'Willaston') they do something even sillier.

Snakes have never been common in Cheshire (Saint Patrick, they say, practised his snake-banishing skills here before embarking for Ireland), so instead of snake charming, we must be content with worm charming. Willaston hosts the annual World Worm Charming Championships. I'm serious.

Every year, on a Saturday in late June, as many as 300 competitors, some from overseas, converge on the village, most of them carrying garden forks, but others lugging hammers, bottles, umbrellas, tennis rackets, cricket bats, drums, trumpets, tubas, xylophones, CD players or bizarre ground-thumping contraptions of their own devising. Worm charming is the mother of invention.

The first World Champion, in 1980, was a local farmer's son, Tom Shufflebotham, who charmed an astonishing 511 worms out of the ground in half an hour. He achieved this – no, not by shuffling his botham – by using the orthodox 'twanging' method with a garden fork.

The rules of the sport were drawn up by the IFCWAP: the International Federation of Charming Worms and Allied Pastimes (what can those 'allied pastimes' be? Seducing snails? Beguiling beetles?). Each team consists of three people: a charmer, a catcher and a counter, and they are restricted to a plot of turf no more than 3 square metres. How you charm the worms is up to you, but no digging is allowed. Another misguided idea is to hide worms up your trousers and let them drop into the grass while the Worm Master is looking the other way. This is sure to be spotted, and once you are disqualified there is no wriggling out of it.

Be careful how you ease them out, as well, because half-worms will not be counted. This is because, contrary to popular belief, the two halves do not grow into independent worms; only the head end can survive, and it may sue.

Some try to tempt them out by pouring water, beer or urine into the grass; others play them recordings of the sound of rainfall or sounds of the sixties such as the Beach Boys' 'Good Vibrations'. Some play instruments, but most resort to thwacking the ground in one way or another. I once saw a father introduce his bemused toddler to the sport by bouncing him up and down on the plot. Tap-dancing has been tried; an idea borrowed from gulls, which 'paddle' with their feet to persuade worms to rise to the surface. Scientific research suggests that the best way to get a worm moving is to imitate the sound of its worst enemy, the mole!

In the 2009 championships, a new star was born. Ten-year-old Sophie Smith of Willaston not only won the coveted Golden Worm trophy, but also got herself into the *Guinness Book of Records*. Her total of 567 worms was achieved entirely without the help of performance-enhancing drugs.

All charmed worms are offered counselling and then released in a secluded spot where, if they get a wiggle on, they are soon safely underground. Until next year, that is!

THE VOICE OF HOME

The artist Charles Tunnicliffe, halfway through his life, left his native Cheshire and moved to the Welsh-speaking island of Anglesey. In 1947, only a few months after settling in, he wrote in his diary:

... a long motor lorry arrived piled up with trees from a nursery in mid-Cheshire. I spoke to the driver and it was indeed pleasant to hear him answer with good Cheshire country speech.

Sale poet H.V. Lucas felt the same way:

... Only a spoken word,
But by an exile
The voice of Home was heard.

Like the smell of new-baked bread, a word or phrase can transport us back to the place and the time of our childhood. But dialect is doubly changeable: it transmutes from place to place and from generation to generation. There is one thing that we all agree on, however: it's dying out, isn't it? There are just a few old speakers left, and when they pop their clogs, that will be it.

Authors have been saying that for a long time. Here, for example, is Peter Wright, in *The Cheshire Chatter* (second edition, 1979):

True, it's changing. Up to 1974 in places like Broken Cross and Tarporley it was easy to find and tape record from free conversation expressions like 'go a-songering' (go reaping), 'ee bees' (hay bays), 'oo's gooin' cauve' (she's going to calve). Today, partly through the influx of visitors, it's harder.

Let us compare that with a book written in 1887: Thomas Darlington's, *The Folk-Speech of South Cheshire*. Then, surely, dialect must have been in a much healthier state, mustn't it? He writes in his introduction:

I have often observed that the very broadest and most thoroughly dialectal pronunciation is to be heard in the playgrounds of our common schools. On the other hand, the vocabulary of the folk-speech has suffered terribly of late years. I am speaking within bounds when I say that above one half of the most characteristic dialect-words recorded hereinafter in the Glossary are never in the mouths of persons under twenty-five, and will consequently be obsolete in another generation. It is no uncommon thing for a boy to be unable to understand words and phrases which his grandfather has used all his life.

A decade earlier, Lt-Col Egerton Leigh had written his *A Glossary of Words Used in the Dialect of Cheshire* (1877). He tells us that he has recorded these words:

> … before the school inspector … should succeed in expatriating, or making penal, any words that might have no dictionary nor polite parlance authority; and before emigration, railways, and the blending of shires, should destroy or expatriate much that is curious and quaint in our CHESHIRISMS.

Sixty years before that, Roger Wilbraham wrote his *Cheshire Glossary* (1817), and compared his findings to John Ray's *A Collection of Words not Generally Used* (1674), and laments the fact that several Cheshire words 'have actually perished since the time of Ray'.

Of course, a thing cannot be on the verge of disappearing for a century and a half!

I suggest that our definition of dialect is cock-eyed. We should think of it as a forest of oak trees that is not so much dying as renewing itself. Every so often an ancient, well-loved tree reaches the end of its life and we lament its passing, but another takes its place and the forest is none the poorer. In reality, we are all dialect speakers, but we take the healthy words for granted and notice only the dying ones.

However, in the next section the reader will receive a short, introductory lesson in South Cheshire dialect as spoken over a century ago. Why? Because, apart from opening a window onto Cheshire's past, it will entertain you and introduce you to some wonderful vocabulary and phraseology.

'I live just opposite them,' is a perfectly adequate phrase, but wouldn't you rather say: '*I live just-a-meet oer-anenst 'em*'?

'Gosh, what a corpulent lady,' sounds feeble next to: 'Laws-a-dees, oo's a bazzil-arsed, bawson swedgel of a woman!'

And when a man lies on his deathbed, can you think of a more poetical phrase than: 'Th' ood mon's gooin' over th' broo'?

As you can see, for beauty, colour and expressiveness, Cheshire knocks Standard English into a cocked hat.

CHESHIRE FOR BEGINNERS

You may be more familiar with dialect than you think. Take this phrase: 'He's nobbut a mardy babby; always mitherin' and chunnerin' about summat or nowt.' Simple enough to understand, but the further we go back in time, the trickier it becomes. A visitor to Delamere in 1874 wrote: 'The dialect here is most trying to strangers. It is almost impossible to understand them at first.' – so don't expect this first lesson to be easy.

As any linguist will tell you, the best way to learn French is to visit France, so we shall go to Crewe and step back in time to the year 1880. It's market day, so we can mingle with the crowd and eavesdrop on the conversations of the market traders and their customers.

First, I must explain how the vowels will be spelt: 'igh' represents the vowel in Received Pronunciation 'mine', 'ey' as in 'main', 'ow' for 'cow', 'oh' for 'low', 'aw' as in 'law'.

A man greets an acquaintance and asks him:

'Didst see Bill upo' th' road?' 'Aye.' 'Nay, tha didna!' 'Yigh, bur ah did!'

'Did you see Bill on the road?' 'Yes.' 'No, you didn't!' 'Yes, I did!'

You notice that there are two words for 'Yes' – 'Aye' when affirming and 'Yigh' when contradicting. 'No' and 'Nay' are distinguished in the same way.

'The', which glides into the following word, is a hard 'th' before a consonant and a soft 'dh' before a vowel (e.g. *upo' th' road, i'dh'edge*).

Didna is one of many negatives whose meanings you can easily guess: *shanna, conna, munna, wunna, dunna, wilna, amna, anna, dostna, hadstna, mustna*, etc.

The two men are evidently workmates, since they use the familiar pronoun '*tha*' rather than '*yey*' (you).

'Well, Tom, shan we ha' reen?
I knowna, but weather's very muttery.'

*'Well, Tom, shall we have rain?
I don't know, but the weather's very dull.'*

Words like rain, day, face and late are pronounced *reen, dee, feece* and *leet*.

'Shall' becomes '*shan*' with a plural pronoun (eg I shall, we *shan*).

'Pon wunna stond theer; I wouldna put th' milk-pon dighn upo'
that kiggly stoo'; I should be feared on it wawtin"

> *'The pan won't stand there; I wouldn't put the milk pan on that
> wobbly stool, I'd be afraid of it overturning.'*

The word 'the' is sometimes left out entirely, so *'Th'pon'*
becomes *'Pon'*.

The final 'L' in words like pool and fool has a habit of
disappearing altogether.

Words like down, house and doubt are pronounced *dighn,
aighce* and *dight*. If Eliza Doolittle had been from Crewe, she
would have recited 'How now, brown cow' and 'the rain in
Spain' as *'High nigh brighn kigh*?' and *'Th'reen i' Speen'*!

> 'If th'ommer binna hisn, hoo-as bin it then?'

> *'If the hammer isn't his, whose is it then?'*

'*Bin*' and '*binna*' are used for 'is' and 'isn't'.

Words like hammer, man and can are pronounced *'ommer,
mon* and *con*.

A portly woman, looking weary and fed up, comes along and
drops her heavy basket on the ground, saying:

> 'I've lommered this basket o' butter to Nantweych an' back, an'
> it's regularly rondlt me up; if yo'n beleyve mey, mester, my back
> aches a-that'n than I con 'ardly shift my legs, an' I'm fit drop
> wi' tire.'

> *'I've lugged this basket of butter to Nantwich and back, and it's
> exhausted me; if you'll believe me, master, my back aches till I
> can hardly shift my legs, and I'm ready to drop for tiredness.'*

The word 'than' (*'than I con 'ardly shift my legs'*) appears to
make no sense, but in Cheshire 'than' and 'till' can exchange
meanings: e.g. 'I work mornin' than neyt; a lot lunger till thee.'

The word 'to' can be omitted, as in 'I'm fit drop wi' tire', or sometimes replaced by 'for' as in *'Tha atna owd enough for go a-womanin'* – You're not old enough to go courting.

'Dunna slat it a-thatuns! That cosses a poweration o' money!'

'Don't throw it down like that! That costs a lot of money!'

A-thatuns, a-thisun, a-which'n, are used for 'like this, like that, like which'.

Words such as costs, crusts, wrists and fists are often pronounced *cosses, crusses, wrisses, fisses*.

'We'n gotten bread enough an' teyters enoo.'

'We have got enough bread and enough potatoes.'

If '*enoo*' and '*enough*' mean the same, why use both? Because, in this dialect, 'enough' is only used with a singular noun, while '*enoo*' is reserved for the plural.

Other words spelt 'ough' can have this 'oo' sound; compare: *'Yon feylt 'anna bin plooed for the memory o' no livin' mon,'* and – *'They won sweyin' backats and forrats on a boo.'*

'I wunna tak ton bight tother.'

'I won't take the one without the other.'

It's getting a little easier, isn't it? Let's leave the market now and give the pub a try. Inside, three old men are sitting at a table in the corner, talking about the landlady's daughter.

'Oo's gone into queyt a bonny woman; an' sich a wheyt-feeced wench as oo was.'

*'She's grown into quite a handsome woman, and she was such a
white-faced girl.'*

'Boy' and 'girl' are unnecessary words – say *lad* and *wench*.

''Er feyther's a regular little 'omnithom of a fella; what con ey do
wi' a great barge of a woman like that for a weyf?'
'Aye, bur 'e's gotten a pocketle o' brass!'

*'Her father's a right little midget of a fellow; what can he do
with a great barge of a woman like that for a wife?'*

A *pocketle* is a pocketful. You may hear folk speak of a *mouthle
o' air*, an *apperntle* (apron-full) *o' teyter-pillin's* (potato-peelings),
a basketle o' peen (peas) or *a bucketle o' wick snigs* (live eels).

''E's no moor sense till a suckin' gonder! 'E was in 'ere thisterdee
– 'E wonna drunk, bur 'e was a bit toddlish – an' oo gen 'im sich
a skerry-coatin' as 'ey ne'er 'ad in 'is life afore.'

*'He has no more sense than a sucking gander! He was in here
yesterday – he wasn't drunk, but he was a bit tipsy – and she
gave him such a scolding as he never had in his life before.'*

'Gen' is the past tense of 'give'.
A young man with a scruffy haircut and broken-down shoes
walks in and tells the barmaid:

'What rotten rubbitch theyse shoon bin! They'm shem-rent
a'ready, an' on'y new a threy-wik ago.'
'Well, ah wudna goo strappuzin' alung a-that'ns, wi' my shoon
unlaced,' she replies.

'What rotten rubbish these shoes are! The soles are ripped already, and only new three weeks ago.'

'Well, I wouldn't go walking sloppily like that, with my shoes unlaced,' she replies.

'Shoon' is the plural of 'shoes'; compare *een* (eyes) and *ighzn* (houses) etc.

'Ah've just seyn Jim Dutton 'im as went to Meriky's weyf,' says the young man. 'I towd 'er, Ah'm gooin' same road as 'im; I'm gooin' oer-run this country, sey if I conna may better ight i' Meriky.'

'I've just seen the wife of Jim Dutton, who went to America.'
'I told her, I going the same way as him; I'm going to get out of this country, see if I can't make better out in America.'

Note that the young man has not met Jim Dutton, but his wife.

'Zowkers, 'oo powd thi yure?' asks one of the older men.
'Ah did.'
'Well, I auvays see, if yer wanten a thing done, yer mun do it yoursel!'

'Who cut your hair?'
'I did.'
'Well, I always say, if you want a thing done, you must do it yourself!'

Certain words beginning with the letter 'h', like hair, head and heat, become *yure*, *yed* and *yet*.

Either *auvays* or *allus* can be used for 'always'.

Mun means 'must', but only in the sense of obligation; otherwise, must is used, e.g. 'Yo mun go, but yo must be a foo.'

The landlady's mother passes through and shows her age by greeting a customer with "Igh bin 'ee?' 'How are you?' In 1880, only the older generation still use this greeting; 'igh bin yer' is more usual by this time. She goes through to the back yard, where she finds her little grandson sitting out in the cold.

> 'Dunna sit cowdin' a-that'ns. Come thy wees within air o' th' fire an' get some warmship, for tha't a poor starft-lookin' little thing.'

> *'Don't sit shivering like that. Come near the fire and get some warmth, for you're a poor, frozen little thing.'*

By *starft-lookin'*, she means that the boy is cold, not hungry. However, he is peckish as well: 'Ah'm welly clemt jeth,' he says, meaning that, like Robert Nixon, he is dying of hunger.

Jeth means 'death' (literally 'to death', but 'to' has been omitted again).

She hands him some leftovers, or *orts* on a plate.

'Ah'm nur gooin' eat yur orts,' says the boy.

She replies: 'Tha wunna clem, lad, as lung as tha con get good orts eat.'

> 'I'm not going to eat your leftovers.'

> *'You won't starve, lad if you can get good leftovers to eat.'*

But now our time machine is beginning to attract attention, so let's leave these good people and return to our own era.

That concludes your first lesson in Cheshire dialect as spoken 140 years ago. Not such a *tatherum-a-dyal* (unintelligible language) as all that, is it?

All the above phrases are borrowed or adapted from those that were noted down by the old researchers: Darlington,

Leigh *et al*. For further reading, seek out their works, but also novels and stories containing Cheshire dialect, such as Beatrice Tunstall's *The Shiny Night*, *Betty Bresskittles* Pattens by James Clough, and the dialect poems of Rowland Egerton Warburton and Hedley Lucas. To hear it spoken, explore the recordings in the British Library Sound Archive. And remember:

Yo'n auvays have a bit o' Cheshire i' yur talk, 'cos it's yur native!

The earliest known reference to the Cheshire Cat is found in Francis Grose's *Dictionary of the Vulgar Tongue* (1788):

CHESHIRE CAT. He grins like a Cheshire Cat; said of anyone who shows his teeth and gums in laughing.